CAHIER

A Beginning

Workbook for

Grammar and

Communication

David M. Stillman, Ph.D.
Ronni L. Gordon, Ph.D.

National Textbook Company
a division of NTC/CONTEMPORARY PUBLISHING GROUP
Lincolnwood, Illinois USA

Editorial Development: Mediatheque Publishers Services, Philadelphia, Pennsylvania

ISBN: 0-8442-1447-7

CONTENTS

PREFACE

Cahier 1: A Beginning Workbook for Grammar and Communication is designed
to provide beginning learners of French with the tools necessary to allow them
to progress most effectively and efficiently through the early stages of study.
Organized into 21 chapters, *Cahier 1* presents concise and well-organized **grammar
explanations** with clear illustrative examples. The **exercises** of *Cahier 1* give learners
of French ample practice with all the basic structures covered by first-year French
textbooks. Most of the exercises are contextualized, thus inviting students to use
their knowledge of French in engaging, communicative situations. **Vocabulary** items
have been chosen to review and expand upon those presented in first-year basal
texts. When an exercise uses words and expressions not commonly found in first-year
textbooks, they are presented and defined before the exercise or defined in the
vocabulary section at the end of the book. Some exercises in *Cahier 1* are built
around **illustrations.** Students practice the grammar point in question by responding
to these attractive visual cues.

Cahier 1 also highlights important features of the French-speaking world in **culture
notes** that help create an authentic context for a particular exercise. Some features
of the French-speaking world presented in the culture boxes include countries
and cities, food and meal schedules, sports, the French city, films, the education
system, and the Francophone world. Progressing from structured to self-expression
exercises, *Cahier 1* offers **Questions personnelles** and/or **Composition** activities
to encourage learners to use the grammatical structures and vocabulary they have
studied to express their own ideas.

Students will find working through *Cahier 1* a rewarding learning experience
because of its easy-to-follow format, the ample space provided to write answers,
and the open and inviting design. Teachers will appreciate the flexible organization
of *Cahier 1,* which allows them to select chapters as necessary to reinforce the
grammar points they are presenting in their classes. The unique integration of all its
features makes *Cahier 1* an engaging, user-friendly workbook that will motivate
learners to communicate and help build confidence in using French. The integrity
of content and format makes *Cahier 1* the perfect fit for every first-year textbook.

Gender and Number of Nouns;
Il y a; Voici/voilà

I. Gender and Number of Nouns; the Definite and Indefinite Articles

■ French nouns are divided into two categories called genders. Nouns are either masculine or feminine. In French, the forms of the articles *(the, a)* are different for masculine and feminine nouns. Study the forms of the French definite article (English *the*).

	masculine		feminine	
singular	le	livre	la	chaise
plural	les	livres	les	chaises

Now study the forms of the indefinite article (English *a, an*).

	masculine		feminine	
singular	un	livre	une	chaise
plural	des	livres	des	chaises

Notes:

1. French has a plural indefinite article, English does not: **des chaises** *chairs.*

2. The plural articles (**les, des**) are the same for both masculine and feminine nouns. The final **-s** is not pronounced unless the noun begins with a vowel, when it is pronounced **z: des‿amis** *friends.*

3. Nouns are made plural by adding **-s.** This **-s** is not pronounced: **des livres** *books.*

4. The definite articles **le** and **la** change to **l'** before nouns beginning with a vowel or a mute **h***: **l'ordinateur** *computer (masc.);* **l'hôtel** *hotel (masc.).*

Dans la classe de français

Masculine nouns	Feminine nouns
le cahier d'exercices *workbook*	**l'affiche** *poster*
le classeur *loose-leaf notebook*	**la carte** *map*
l'ordinateur *computer*	**la cassette** *cassette, tape*

---

*The letter **h** is silent in French. With a few exceptions, words beginning with **h** are treated as though they begin with a vowel.

A. Articles. Complete the following charts for each noun according to the model.

			definite	*indefinite*
Modèle	livre	singular	le livre	un livre
		plural	les livres	des livres

1. affiche

	definite	*indefinite*
singular	_____	_____
plural	_____	_____

2. classeur

	definite	*indefinite*
singular	_____	_____
plural	_____	_____

3. crayon

	definite	*indefinite*
singular	_____	_____
plural	_____	_____

4. carte

	definite	*indefinite*
singular	_____	_____
plural	_____	_____

5. ordinateur

	definite	*indefinite*
singular	_____	_____
plural	_____	_____

Le système scolaire

■ The French school system has three major divisions: **école primaire, collège, lycée.** Students attend the école primaire (elementary school) for five years and then the collège for three years.

■ After the collège, students enter the lycée for three years. There are two kinds of lycées, academic and technical.

■ In the collège and lycée, French students take as many as ten subjects, but each class does not meet every day.

II. *Il y a*

- The phrase **il y a** means *there is* or *there are*. It can be used before both singular and plural nouns. Most of the time, the indefinite article (**un, une, des**) is used after **il y a** before the noun that follows.

  Il y a un jardin derrière la maison. *There's a garden behind the house.*

  Il y a des voitures devant la maison. *There are cars in front of the house.*

III. Prepositions

- Some common prepositions

  à *at, to*   **derrière** *in back of, behind*

  de *from, of*   **devant** *in front of*

  dans *in*   **sous** *under*

  entre *between*   **sur** *on*

- The prepositions **à** and **de** contract with the definite articles **le** and **les**.

  à + le ➤ **au**   de + le ➤ **du**

  à + les ➤ **aux**   de + les ➤ **des**

- There are no contractions with the definite articles **la** and **l'**.

  au magasin *at the store*   **du** magasin *from the store*

  à la maison *at home*   **de la** maison *from home*

  à l'école *at school*   **de l'**école *from school*

  aux magasins *at the stores* **des** magasins *from the stores*

- Some French prepositions consist of several words ending in **de**. The **de** contracts with the definite articles **le** and **les**.

  à côté de *next to*   **près du** magasin *near the store*

  en face de *opposite, across from*   **près de l'**école *near the school*

  près de *near*   **près des** salles de classe
                                      near the classrooms

  loin de *far from*

- The preposition plus the noun that follows it is called a prepositional phrase. **Sur le bureau noir** and **devant l'école** are prepositional phrases.

B. La chambre de Marie-Laure. Look at the picture of Marie-Laure's room. Then describe the location of the objects indicated using **il y a** + a prepositional phrase.

La chambre de Marie-Laure

la corbeille *wastebasket*

l'étagère *(fem.) bookcase*

le fauteuil *armchair, easy chair*

le magnétophone *tape player*

le mur *wall*

le parquet *floor*

la revue *magazine*

le sac à dos *backpack*

Modèle   sac à dos/chaise *(on)*
➢ Il y a un sac à dos sur la chaise.

1. crayons/bureau *(on)*

_____

2. cassettes/magnétophone *(next to)*

_____

3. bicyclette/porte *(in front of)*

_____

4. lampe/lit et fauteuil *(between)*

   _____

5. chat/chaise *(under)*

   _____

6. papiers/corbeille *(in)*

   _____

IV. Negative of *il y a*

- The negative of **il y a** is **il n'y a pas** *(there isn't, there aren't)*. After a negative, the indefinite article changes to **de** (**d'** before a vowel or mute **h**).

Il n'y a pas de crayons dans le sac à dos.	*There are no (There aren't any) pencils in the backpack.*
Il n'y a pas d'ordinateur sur le bureau.	*There's no (There isn't any) computer on the desk.*

C. Il n'y a pas de... Now describe Marie-Laure's room by telling what is not in it. Follow the model.

Modèle ordinateur/étagère *(on)*
> ➤ Il n'y a pas d'ordinateur sur l'étagère.

1. chien/porte *(behind)*

   _____

2. poste de télé/fauteuil *(facing, opposite)*

   _____

3. calculatrice/sac à dos *(in)*

   _____

4. vêtements/lit *(on)*

   _____

5. table/lit *(near)*

   _____

6. papiers/chaise *(under)*

   _____

V. *Voici, voilà*

- **Voici** and **voilà** are used to point to things. Both words are used before singular and plural nouns. **Voici** means *here is, here are* and **voilà** means *there is, there are*. In everyday French, **voilà** usually replaces **voici**, so **voilà** can mean *here is, here are* as well as *there is, there are*.

Voici l'école.	*Here's the school.*
Voilà les magasins.	*There are the stores.* (also, *Here are the stores.*)

D. La visite de l'école. Lisette is showing her friend Marianne around her school. Each time Marianne asks about something using **il y a,** Lisette points it out using **voilà.**

Modèle   (salles de classe) ➤
Marianne: Il y a des salles de classe?
Lisette: Voilà les salles de classe.

1. bibliothèque

    Marianne: _____

    Lisette: _____

2. gymnases

    Marianne: _____

    Lisette: _____

3. laboratoire de langues

    Marianne: _____

    Lisette: _____

4. cantine *(lunchroom)*

    Marianne: _____

    Lisette: _____

5. salle de réunion *(auditorium)*

    Marianne: _____

    Lisette: _____

6. terrain de sport *(sports field)*

Marianne: _____

Lisette: _____

VI. Uses of the Preposition *de*

■ The preposition **de** is used to indicate possession in French. English often uses *'s* or *s'* to indicate possession. There is no equivalent of these endings in French.

les livres **de** Suzanne   *Suzanne's books*

le bureau **des** professeurs   *the teachers' office*

■ The preposition **de** is used to join two nouns together. Note that the English translations of these phrases consist of two nouns with no preposition. No article is used after **de** in this construction. **De** changes to **d'** before a vowel or a mute **h.**

le magasin *store* + les vêtements *clothing* ➤
le magasin de vêtements *clothing store*

la classe *class* + l'anglais *English (language)* ➤
la classe d'anglais *English class*

E. C'est à qui? One friend notices certain objects. The other tells her whose they are. Use the cues given to write an exchange about each thing.

Modèle   livre/Suzanne ➤
         —Il y a un livre ici.
         —Ah, oui, le livre de Suzanne.

1. cahier/professeur

_____

_____

2. jouets *(toys)*/enfants

_____

_____

3. sac à dos/Louis

_____

_____

➤➤➤➤➤

4. ordinateur/secrétaires

_____

_____

5. classeurs/étudiants

_____

_____

6. parking/école

_____

_____

Être and avoir

I. The Present Tense of the Verb *être* (to be)

■ Study the conjugation of **être** *(to be)*. Notice the personal pronouns and the verb forms.

ÊTRE *TO BE*

	singular			plural		
first person	je	suis	*I am*	nous	sommes	*we are*
second person	tu	es	*you are*	vous	êtes	*you are*
third person	il	est	*he, it is*	ils	sont	*they are*
	elle	est	*she, it is*	elles	sont	*they are*

Notes:

1. French has two words for *you*. The pronoun **tu** is informal singular. The pronoun **vous** can be singular or plural. When it is used to address one person, it is a formal way of saying *you*. **Vous** is also used to address more than one person, both formally and informally.

2. The pronouns **il** and **elle** refer to both people and things. All masculine nouns are referred to as **il;** all feminine nouns are referred to as **elle.**

3. French has two pronouns that are the equivalent of English *they*. **Ils** refers to groups of males or groups consisting of both males and females. **Elles** refers to groups of females only.

A. Quels sujets? Check all the possible subjects each form of **être** corresponds to.

1. es

   je _____ tu _____ il _____ elle _____ nous _____ vous _____ ils _____ elles _____

2. sommes

   je _____ tu _____ il _____ elle _____ nous _____ vous _____ ils _____ elles _____

3. sont

   je _____ tu _____ il _____ elle _____ nous _____ vous _____ ils _____ elles _____

4. est

   je _____ tu _____ il _____ elle _____ nous _____ vous _____ ils _____ clles _____

5. suis

   je _____ tu _____ il _____ elle _____ nous _____ vous _____ ils _____ elles _____

B. Où? Tell where the following people and things are by completing these sentences with the correct form of **être.**

1. Jacques _____ à l'école.

2. Les livres _____ sur l'étagère.

3. Je _____ avec mes parents.

4. Le professeur _____ devant la classe.

5. Nous _____ dans la salle de classe.

6. Tu _____ au laboratoire de langues.

7. Marie et Diane? Elles _____ à la maison.

8. Vous _____ à côté de la fenêtre.

C. Les pronoms. Complete the following exchanges with the correct pronoun.

1. —Où est le chat?

   —_____ est sous le lit.

2. —Tu es dans la chambre?

   —Non, _____ suis dans le jardin.

3. —Où est la calculatrice?

   —_____ est sur le bureau.

4. —Où sont les cassettes?

   —_____ sont derrière le magnétophone.

5. —Vous êtes à l'école?

   —Non, _____ sommes au magasin.

6. —Où est la bibliothèque?

   —_____ est près de la cantine.

7. —Où sont les chiens?

   —_____ sont devant la maison.

8. —Je suis dans la classe de français?

   —Non, _____ êtes dans la classe d'anglais.

D. Où sont les amis? Write exchanges about where these people are. Remember to make the necessary contractions of the preposition **à** and the definite article.

Modèle   Barbara/bibliothèque ➤
            —Où est Barbara?
            —Elle est à la bibliothèque.

1. Philippe et Marc/piscine *(pool)*

    _____

    _____

2. Élisabeth/aéroport

    _____

    _____

3. les amis/cinéma

    _____

    _____

4. Caroline et Françoise/théâtre

    _____

    _____

5. Charles/stade *(stadium)*

    _____

    _____

Dans une ville française

As you walk around a French city, you may discover the following:

■ **Maison des Jeunes et de la Culture.** A community center that has sports and cultural facilities and that often sponsors theater, music, and dance performances.

■ **Auberge de la Jeunesse.** A Youth Hostel, a chain of establishments that provides inexpensive lodging for travelers. They are located in most cities and in many rural areas.

■ **Syndicat d'initiative.** Located throughout the country, the Syndicat d'initiative has brochures and maps about every facet of France that could be interesting to a visitor.

II. *C'est, ce sont*

■ The phrases **c'est** and **ce sont** are used to identify people or things. They are most often followed by an article + a noun or by a proper noun (a name of a person or place). **C'est** is used before singular nouns and **ce sont** is used before plural nouns, although in everyday speech, **c'est** may replace **ce sont** before plurals.

C'est une école.	*It's a school.*
Ce sont des cinémas.	*Those are movie theaters.*
C'est le professeur.	*It's the teacher.*
Ce sont les professeurs d'anglais.	*It's the English teachers.*

■ The negative of these constructions are **ce n'est pas** and **ce ne sont pas**. After the negative of **être**, the indefinite articles **un, une, des** do not change to **de**.

Ce n'est pas le professeur.	*It's not the teacher.*
Ce ne sont pas des cinémas.	*Those are not movie theaters.*
(Compare: **Il n'y a pas de cinémas.**	*There are no movie theaters.*)

■ Both **c'est** and **il est/elle est** can be used to tell what someone's job or profession is. When **c'est** is used the indefinite article is also used. When **il est/elle est** is used, the noun follows **est** directly.

C'est un médecin.	*It's a doctor. He's a doctor. She's a doctor.*
Il est médecin.	*He's a doctor.*
Elle est médecin.	*She's a doctor.*

E. **C'est qui?** Write exchanges between two friends in which one corrects the other's impression about who certain people are. **Là-bas** means *there* or *over there*.

Les gens

l'homme *(masc.) man*	**le professeur** *teacher (male or female)*
la femme *woman*	
l'avocat *(male) lawyer*	**le programmeur** *(male) programmer*
l'avocate *(female) lawyer*	
le client *(male) customer*	**la programmeuse** *(female) programmer*
la cliente *(female) customer*	
l'étudiant *(male) student*	**le secrétaire** *(male) secretary*
l'étudiante *(female) student*	**la secrétaire** *(female) secretary*
le médecin *doctor (male or female)*	**le vendeur** *(male) salesclerk*
	la vendeuse *(female) salesclerk*

Modèle un homme/un étudiant/un professeur ➤
        —Il y a un homme là-bas. C'est un étudiant?
        —Non, ce n'est pas un étudiant. C'est un professeur.

1. un homme/un avocat/un médecin

    _____

    _____

2. une femme/la vendeuse/la cliente

    _____

    _____

3. un homme/un professeur/un programmeur

    _____

    _____

4. une femme/une programmeuse/une avocate

    _____

    _____

5. un homme/un secrétaire/un client

    _____

    _____

F. **Quelle profession?** Complete each of the following sentences with **c'est, il est,** or **elle est.**

1. _____ une avocate.   5. _____ vendeur.

2. _____ professeur d'anglais.   6. _____ étudiante.

3. _____ programmeur.   7. _____ un étudiant.

4. _____ une programmeuse.   8. _____ une secrétaire.

III. The Present Tense of the Verb *avoir* (to have)

■ Study the conjugation of **avoir** *(to have)*.

AVOIR *TO HAVE*

	singular			plural		
first person	j'	ai	*I have*	nous	avons	*we have*
second person	tu	as	*you have*	vous	avez	*you have*
third person	il	a	*he, it has*	ils	ont	*they have*
	elle	a	*she, it has*	elles	ont	*they have*

Notes:

1. The pronoun **je** becomes **j'** before a vowel, as in **j'ai.**

2. All the plural forms of **avoir** have a **liaison.** The final **s** of the pronouns is pronounced as /z/. Be sure to distinguish **ils_ont, elles_ont** from **ils sont, elles sont** in pronunciation. The forms for *they have* (**ils_ont, elles_ont**) have a /z/ sound in **liaison.** The forms for *they are* (**ils sont, elles sont**) have an /s/ sound.

G. À relier. Link the verb forms in column B to their subjects in column A.

A

_____ 1. avez

_____ 2. as

_____ 3. avons

_____ 4. ont

_____ 5. ai

_____ 6. a

B

a. j'

b. il

c. elles

d. vous

e. nous

f. tu

H. Quels sujets? Check all the possible subjects each form of **avoir** corresponds to.

1. a

   j'_____ tu _____ il _____ elle _____ nous _____ vous _____ ils _____ elles _____

2. avez

   j'_____ tu _____ il _____ elle _____ nous _____ vous _____ ils _____ elles _____

3. ont

   j'_____ tu _____ il _____ elle _____ nous _____ vous _____ ils _____ elles _____

4. as

   j'_____ tu _____ il _____ elle _____ nous _____ vous _____ ils _____ elles _____

5. ai

   j'____ tu ____ il ____ elle ____ nous ____ vous ____ ils ____ elles ____

6. avons

   j'____ tu ____ il ____ elle ____ nous ____ vous ____ ils ____ elles ____

I. Les choses. What gadgets and devices do the students have? Tell what they have using the correct form of the verb **avoir.**

Les choses

l'appareil-photo *(masc.) camera*   **le disque compact** *compact disc*

le baladeur (le walkman) *walkman*   **l'imprimante** *(fem.) printer*

la caméra *camcorder, movie camera*   **la mobylette** *moped*

la chaîne-stéréo *stereo*   **le répondeur** *answering machine*

Modèle   Elvire/chaîne-stéréo
   ➤ Elvire a une chaîne-stéréo.

1. les étudiants/baladeurs

   _____

2. je/vélo

   _____

3. Suzanne et Claire/disques compacts

   _____

4. Luc/une mobylette

   _____

5. tu/imprimante

   _____

6. nous/caméras

   _____

➤➤➤➤➤

7. vous/répondeur

_____

8. le professeur/appareil-photo

_____

J. Conversation sur les objets. One friend asks if people have certain things. The other friend says that they do and tells the person asking where they are. Write what they say to each other.

Modèle Jacques/classeur/sur/table ➢
  —Jacques a un classeur?
  —Oui, il est sur la table.

1. Anne et Christine/disques compacts/à côté de/chaîne-stéréo

_____

_____

2. M. Gilbert/voiture/devant/maison

_____

_____

3. les étudiants/mobylettes/dans/parking

_____

_____

4. Pierre/chat/dans/fauteuil

_____

_____

5. tu/affiches/à/mur

_____

_____

6. vous/cartes de France/sur/étagère

_____

_____

7. le professeur/imprimante/sous/ordinateur

_____

_____

8. Serge et Fanny/vélos/dans/jardin

_____

_____

_____

K. **Composition.** Describe your room, the objects in it, and their location in a paragraph of five or six sentences. Use phrases such as **Dans ma chambre il y a...**, **J'ai un/une...**, **Il/Elle est...**, etc.

-Er Verbs

I. Verbs Ending in *-er*

■ Study the endings of the verbs ending in -er.

PARLER *TO SPEAK*

singular		plural	
je	parle	nous	parlons
tu	parles	vous	parlez
il/elle	parle	ils/elles	parlent
on	parle		

Notes:

1. The pronoun **on** in French means *one, people,* or even *you* or *they* when the meaning is *you* or *they* in general.

   Ici **on parle** français.   *People speak* French here; French *is spoken* here.

   On écoute le professeur.   *You/We/They/People listen* to the teacher.

2. The pronoun **je** becomes **j'** before a vowel or a mute **h.**

   j'arrive, **j'**étudie, **j'**habite

3. In spite of the differences in spelling, all the singular forms (**je, tu, il**) of -**er** verbs and the third-person plural form (**ils, elles**) sound alike.

4. The present tense of French verbs has several meanings in English.

   Ils travaillent en ville.   { *They work downtown.*
{ *They are working downtown.*

   In questions, the French verb covers the meaning of English *do* or *does.*

   Ils travaillent en ville?   *Do they work downtown?*

■ Some useful -**er** verbs

aimer *to like, to love*	**dessiner** *to draw*	**habiter** *to live (reside)*
apporter *to bring*	**détester** *to hate*	**parler** *to speak*
arriver *to arrive*	**dîner** *to have dinner*	**passer** *to spend time*
chanter *to sing*	**entrer** *to enter, come in*	**travailler** *to work*
danser *to dance*	**étudier** *to study*	**trouver** *to find*
déjeuner *to have lunch*	**fermer** *to close*	

A. À relier. Match the verbs in column B with their subjects in column A. Each form can be used only once.

A

_____ 1. je

_____ 2. vous

_____ 3. Gérard

_____ 4. elles

_____ 5. tu

_____ 6. nous

B

a. trouves

b. est

c. ferme

d. détestons

e. chantent

f. dessinez

B. Quels sujets? Check all the possible subjects each verb form corresponds to.

1. passes

   je ___ tu ___ il ___ elle ___ on ___ nous ___ vous ___ ils ___ elles ___

2. habitez

   je ___ tu ___ il ___ elle ___ on ___ nous ___ vous ___ ils ___ elles ___

3. parlent

   je ___ tu ___ il ___ elle ___ on ___ nous ___ vous ___ ils ___ elles ___

4. aimes

   je ___ tu ___ il ___ elle ___ on ___ nous ___ vous ___ ils ___ elles ___

5. travaille

   je ___ tu ___ il ___ elle ___ on ___ nous ___ vous ___ ils ___ elles ___

6. apportent

   je ___ tu ___ il ___ elle ___ on ___ nous ___ vous ___ ils ___ elles ___

7. entrons

   je ___ tu ___ il ___ elle ___ on ___ nous ___ vous ___ ils ___ elles ___

8. danse

   je ___ tu ___ il ___ elle ___ on ___ nous ___ vous ___ ils ___ elles ___

C. Les étudiants. There are many students from abroad at summer school. Tell what language each one speaks using the verb **parler.**

Modèle Gary/anglais
> ➤ Gary parle anglais.

1. Jacqueline/français _____

2. Hans et Ursula/allemand _____

3. je/anglais _____

4. vous/espagnol _____

5. Shu-Ling et Ren-Wei/chinois _____

6. tu/italien _____

D. Quand est-ce qu'on arrive? Ask when each person is arriving.

Modèle Paulette/aujourd'hui
> ➤ Paulette arrive aujourd'hui?

Expressions de temps

à l'heure *on time, punctually*	aujourd'hui *today*
en avance *early (ahead of time)*	demain *tomorrow*
en retard *late*	la semaine prochaine *next week*

1. Marc et François/lundi

_____

2. vous/demain

_____

3. Christine/samedi

_____

4. tu/mardi

_____

5. Luc et Mireille/la semaine prochaine

_____

6. le professeur/en avance

_____

7. je/à l'heure

_____

8. nous/en retard

_____

II. Verbs and Their Objects

■ Some **-er** verbs in French are not followed by prepositions (words like *for, to, at*) the way their English equivalents are.

chercher un livre	*to look for a book*
chercher un restaurant	*to look for a restaurant*
écouter une chanson	*to listen to a song*
écouter la radio	*to listen to the radio*
regarder la télé	*to watch (look at) television*
regarder des photos	*to look at pictures (photographs)*
regarder le tableau noir	*to look at the chalkboard*
—Est-ce que **tu regardes** la télé aujourd'hui?	*Are you watching TV today?*
—Non, **j'écoute** la radio.	*No, I'm listening to the radio.*

■ The verb **entrer,** however, is always followed by the preposition **dans** before a noun.

Nous **entrons dans** la salle de classe.	*We **enter** the classroom.*

■ The verb **jouer** *(to play)* is followed by the preposition **à** before the name of a game or sport.

jouer aux cartes, aux dames, aux échecs	*to play cards, checkers, chess*
jouer au football, au basket(-ball), au morpion	*to play soccer, basketball, tic-tac-toe*
jouer à la balle	*to play ball*

■ The preposition **de** is used before the name of a musical instrument.

jouer du piano, du violon, du saxophone	*to play the piano, the violin, the saxophone*
jouer de la flûte, de la guitare, de la clarinette	*to play the flute, the guitar, the clarinet*
jouer de l'alto, de l'accordéon	*to play the viola, the accordion*

E. Après le dîner. You go to see the Lemeunier family after dinner. Tell what each person is doing when you arrive.

Modèle   Madame Lemeunier/préparer/le café
➤ Madame Lemeunier prépare le café.

1. je/arriver/à la porte

_____

2. je/entrer/la maison

_____

3. Madame Lemeunier/regarder/le journal

_____

4. Jean-Luc/écouter/une cassette

_____

5. les grands-parents/jouer/cartes

_____

6. Jean et Cécile/regarder/la télé

_____

7. Suzanne Lemeunier/jouer/la guitare

_____

8. Monsieur Lemeunier/apporter/le café

_____

F. On joue! Tell what games and instruments this group of friends is playing. Add the correct preposition and article to each sentence.

1. Richard et ses amis jouent _____ base-ball.

2. Marc joue _____ guitare.

3. Odile joue _____ volley-ball avec Mireille.

4. Josette et Catherine jouent _____ handball.

5. Mimi joue _____ flûte.

6. Au Canada on joue beaucoup _____ hockey.

7. Sylvie et Georges jouent _____ dames.

8. Gérard et Pierre jouent _____ échecs.

G. Avant la classe. The teacher is late today. To find out what's going on in class, create sentences out of each string of words.

Modèle   le professeur/arriver/en retard/aujourd'hui
➤ Le professeur arrive en retard aujourd'hui.

1. Marc et Lucie/regarder/une revue

   _____

2. Paul/parler/avec Georges

   _____

3. tu/étudier/pour l'examen

   _____

4. nous/dessiner/dans nos cahiers

   _____

5. je/chanter/avec Renée

   _____

6. (Claude et toi) vous/jouer/le morpion

   _____

7. le professeur/entrer/la salle de classe

   _____

8. nous/chercher/nos livres

   _____

Les sports

- The most popular sport in France is soccer, called **le football.** Most French cities have a soccer team, and the French national championship is called the **Championnat de France.** A national French all-star team also participates in the World Cup match (**la Coupe du monde**). Baseball and American football are rarely played.
- Cycling as a competitive sport is very popular in France. The yearly **Tour de France,** a national bicycle race of nearly 2500 kilometers, attracts cyclists from all over the world.
- Other popular sports in France are skiing, rugby, tennis, and, for spectators, horse-racing and auto-racing.

H. Une bonne classe de français. Mme Gervais is an excellent French teacher. Complete this paragraph with the correct present tense forms of the verbs in parentheses to find out what her class is like.

La classe de français

enseigner *to teach*   **saluer** *to greet, to say hello to*

imiter *to imitate*   **l'histoire** *(fem.) story*

inventer *to invent, to make up*   **le jeu** (*plural:* **les jeux**) *game*

présenter *to present, to introduce*   **la leçon** *lesson*

raconter *to tell, to narrate*   **la prononciation** *pronunciation*

Mme Gervais _____ (1. être) professeur de français. Elle

_____ (2. enseigner) dans un lycée. Je _____ (3. être)

étudiant dans sa classe. Quand elle _____ (4. entrer) dans la salle de

classe, elle _____ (5. saluer) les étudiants. Elle _____

(6. présenter) la leçon. Nous _____ (7. imiter) sa prononciation.

Elle _____ (8. raconter) des histoires en français et les étudiants

_____ (9. écouter) avec attention. Parfois *(sometimes)* nous

_____ (10. inventer) des jeux en français. Nous _____

(11. aimer) la classe de français.

I. Composition. Imagine you're spending a wonderful day with your friends. Describe in five or six sentences what you are doing, what games or sports you are playing, etc.

Negatives and Questions

I. Negatives

■ French verbs are made negative by placing **ne** before the verb and **pas** after it. **Ne** changes to **n'** if the verb begins with a vowel or a mute **h.**

Nous **ne** travaillons **pas** aujourd'hui.   *We're **not** working today.*

Il **n'**étudie **pas** à la bibliothèque.   *He **doesn't** study (is **not** studying) at the library.*

■ After a negative, the indefinite articles (**un, une, des**) become **de** (unless the verb is **être**).

Je regarde **un** film. ➢ Je **ne** regarde **pas de** film.

Nous avons **des** cassettes. ➢ Nous **n'**avons **pas de** cassettes.

A. La flemme *(Laziness).* Nobody feels like doing much of anything today. Tell what people are not doing using the negative.

Modèle   Luc/jouer aux échecs
➢ Luc ne joue pas aux échecs.

1. Janine/étudier le français

_____

2. tu/chercher des livres à la bibliothèque

_____

3. Nicole et Vincent/dîner dans un restaurant

_____

4. nous/jouer au football

_____

5. le professeur/arriver à l'heure

_____

6. vous/dessiner

_____

➢➢➢➢➢

7. Frédéric et Zoë/danser

_____

8. je/travailler

_____

B. **Qui étudie? Personne.** Sophie wants to know if people are studying today. Tell her in each case that they are not and what they are doing instead.

Modèle —Maurice étudie aujourd'hui? (travailler au magasin)
➢ —Non, il n'étudie pas. Il travaille au magasin.

1. —Virginie et Laure étudient aujourd'hui? (passer l'après-midi au parc)

— _____

2. —Bertrand étudie aujourd'hui? (écouter des cassettes)

— _____

3. —Claude et toi, vous étudiez aujourd'hui? (regarder un film à la télé)

— _____

4. —Véronique étudie aujourd'hui? (jouer au tennis)

— _____

5. —Tu étudies aujourd'hui? (dîner au restaurant)

— _____

6. —J'étudie aujourd'hui? (jouer aux dames avec moi)

— _____

C. **La bonne conduite.** Use the subject pronoun **on** and a negative to explain what is considered good conduct in Madame Arnaud's classe.

Modèle parler avec les amis
➢ On ne parle pas avec les amis.

1. dessiner dans son livre de français

_____

2. regarder par la fenêtre

_____

3. arriver en retard

_____

4. jouer au morpion

_____

5. apporter son chat

_____

6. rêver *(to dream, daydream)* en classe

_____

D. Quand on est libre. What do you and your friends do in your free time or during vacations? Tell whether or not you do these activities often (**souvent**). Note the position of the word **souvent** in the model.

Modèle   écouter la radio
       ➤ Mes amis et moi, nous écoutons souvent la radio.
      or
      ➤ Mes amis et moi, nous n'écoutons pas souvent la radio.

1. skier

_____

2. regarder la télé

_____

3. dessiner ensemble

_____

4. visiter les musées de la ville

_____

5. jouer au tennis

_____

6. dîner au restaurant

_____

II. Questions

- The simplest way to ask a question in French is to raise the pitch of the voice at the end of a sentence.

Paulette habite près du lycée.	*Paulette lives near the high school.*
Paulette habite près du lycée?	*Does Paulette live near the high school?*

- Another way to ask a question is to add the phrase **Est-ce que** at the beginning of a statement. **Est-ce que** becomes **Est-ce qu'** before a vowel or a mute **h.**

Est-ce que le professeur est là?	*Is the teacher here?*
Est-ce qu'il est dans la salle de classe?	*Is he in the classroom?*

- Question words are used with **est-ce que.** Here are some common question words.

comment? *how?*	**quand?** *when?*
où? *where?*	**qui?** *who? (subject of the verb)*
pourquoi? *why?*	**qui est-ce que?** *whom? (object of the verb)*
qu'est-ce que? *what?*	

Où est-ce que tu habites?	*Where do you live?*
Qu'est-ce que vous regardez?	*What are you looking at?*
Qui travaille ici?	*Who works here?*
Qui est-ce que vous cherchez?	*Whom are you looking for?*

- Questions can also be negative.

Qui n'étudie **pas** aujourd'hui?	*Who is **not** studying today?*
Pourquoi est-ce que vous n'écoutez **pas**?	*Why aren't you listening?*

E. Qu'est-ce que? Ask what these people are doing. Use **qu'est-ce que.**

Modèle   Jean/chanter
   ➤ Qu'est-ce que Jean chante?

1. Guillaume et Paul/chercher

   _____

2. vous/regarder

   _____

3. Nathalie/parle

_____

4. tu/dessiner

_____

5. nous/étudier aujourd'hui

_____

6. elles/préparer

_____

F. Comment? Ask how these people find certain things. Use the verb **trouver** as in the model.

Modèle   Alain/la classe de français
➤ Comment est-ce qu'Alain trouve la classe de français?

1. tu/le film

_____

2. les étudiants/le livre d'anglais

_____

3. il/le professeur de maths

_____

4. Monique/la chambre

_____

5. les enfants/la bicyclette

_____

6. Monsieur Rémy/la voiture

_____

G. Où ça? Find out where these people do certain things. Follow the model.

Modèle   vous/dîner
> ➤ Où est-ce que vous dînez?

1. Mlle Martel/travailler

_____

2. elle/déjeuner

_____

3. les étudiants/étudier

_____

4. vous/jouer au tennis

_____

5. les amis/danser

_____

6. elles/habiter

_____

H. Alors? Your friend tells you something that is not true. Ask a question to find out what the facts are.

Modèle   Philippe n'aime pas Brigitte. *(Ask whom.)*
> ➤ Qui est-ce qu'il aime alors?

1. Le professeur n'arrive pas maintenant. *(Ask when.)*

_____

2. Jeanne ne travaille pas ici. *(Ask where.)*

_____

3. Les étudiants n'écoutent pas les cassettes. *(Ask what.)*

_____

4. Marc ne joue pas bien. *(Ask how.)*

_____

5. Odile et Janine ne cherchent pas Mme Maurois. *(Ask whom.)*

_____

6. Je ne parle pas anglais avec Hélène. *(Ask what.)*

   _____

7. François n'habite pas ici. *(Ask who.)*

   _____

8. Charles et moi, nous ne dînons pas au restaurant. *(Ask where.)*

   _____

I. Le nouveau professeur. Monsieur Poiret is talking to a new teacher at the **lycée.** Write out the questions Monsieur Poiret asks to get to know him. Use the words given and ask the questions in the **vous** form.

Modèle   comment/trouver le lycée
   ➤ Comment est-ce que vous trouvez le lycée?

1. où/habiter

   _____

2. pourquoi/arriver en avance

   _____

3. qui/travailler avec vous

   _____

4. qu'est-ce que/apporter pour le déjeuner

   _____

5. quand/quitter *(to leave)* le lycée aujourd'hui

   _____

6. qu'est-ce que/chercher sur l'étagère

   _____

7. pourquoi/ne pas déjeuner à la cantine

   _____

8. qu'est-ce que/ne pas aimer ici

   _____

J. Qu'est-ce qu'ils ont? Create conversational exchanges about the things these students have and don't have. Follow the model.

Modèle Françoise/mobylette/vélo ➤
  —Est-ce que Françoise a une mobylette?
  —Non, elle n'a pas de mobylette. Elle a un vélo.

1. Luc et Paul/cassettes/disques compacts

   _____

   _____

2. tu/chaîne-stéréo/baladeur

   _____

   _____

3. Julie/classeur/cahier d'exercices

   _____

   _____

4. la salle de classe/ordinateurs/magnétophones

   _____

   _____

5. l'école/terrain de sport/gymnase *(masc.)*

   _____

   _____

6. vous/fauteuil/chaises

   _____

   _____

7. Bertrand/voiture/bicyclette

   _____

   _____

8. M. et Mme Chevalier/caméra/appareil-photo

_____

_____

III. *N'est-ce pas?*

■ The phrase **n'est-ce pas** can be added to statements to turn them into questions. Questions with **n'est-ce pas** imply that the person asking expects the answer *yes*. Compare the "tags" that are the equivalent of **n'est-ce pas** in the English translations.

Il est souvent en retard, **n'est-ce pas?**	*He's often late, **isn't he**?*
Elles travaillent en ville, **n'est-ce pas?**	*They work downtown, **don't they**?*
Ce sont des étudiants, **n'est-ce pas?**	*They're students, **aren't they**?*

K. N'est-ce pas? Check to see if these things are true by creating questions ending in **n'est-ce pas.**

Modèle   Louise/parler français
➤ Louise parle français, n'est-ce pas?

1. tu/étudier aujourd'hui

_____

2. Marc et Lucille/être à la cantine

_____

3. je/avoir une classe d'histoire maintenant

_____

4. vous/travailler à l'aéroport

_____

5. l'école/être près du stade

_____

6. M. Malmaison/enseigner le français

_____

➤➤➤➤➤

7. nous/jouer au football

_____

8. Sara et Christine/chercher un restaurant

_____

L. Pas exactement. Your friend asks you questions using **n'est-ce pas,** but is mistaken about what she sees. Use the cues given to write her question and correct her impressions based on the drawings. Use dashes to indicate that you are writing a conversation between two people.

Modèle Philippe et Roger/jouer aux cartes ➤
—Philippe et Roger jouent aux cartes, n'est-ce pas?
—Non, ils jouent au basket-ball.

1. le chat/sur la chaise

— _____

_____

— _____

2. les copains/être au gymnase

— _____

_____

— _____

3. Marguerite et Lise/regarder des photos

— _____

_____

— _____

4. Richard/jouer du piano

— _____

_____

— _____

5. ce sont/avocats

— _____

_____

— _____

Le film et le théâtre

- **Le film.** France is a major movie-producing country, and movies are popular in France. France produces between 100 and 150 films a year, and French studios such as **Gaumont** and **Pathé** are famous. American movies are also very popular in France and make up nearly 60% of the market.
- **Le théâtre.** The French theater is a combination of government-subsidized and private enterprises. Among the government-sponsored theaters is the **Comédie Française,** created by Louis XIV in 1680. The Comédie Française specializes in the French classics.

M. Composition. Write an eight-sentence dialogue between two students who are getting to know each other at the beginning of the school year. One student should ask the other about what he or she likes, what things he or she has, what his or her room is like, and who his or her friends are.

Plural of Nouns and Adjectives; Agreement and Position of Adjectives

I. Plural of Nouns and Adjectives

■ Nouns and adjectives in French are made plural by adding **-s.** This letter is usually silent. In speech, it is the change in the form of the article that indicates that a noun is plural. There are some exceptions to the use of **-s** to form the plural.

   a. Nouns and adjectives ending in **-s** or **-x** in the singular do not add **-s** to form the plural.

     le fils *son* ➤ **les fils** *sons*

     un repas délicieux *a delicious meal* ➤
     des repas délicieux *delicious meals*

   b. Nouns and adjectives ending in **-eau** and nouns ending in **-eu** add **-x,** not **-s,** to form the plural.

     un nouveau bateau *a new boat* ➤ **des nouveaux bateaux** *new boats*

     le jeu *game* ➤ **les jeux** *games*

   c. Most nouns ending in **-al** or **-ail** change the **-al** or **-ail** to **-aux** to form the plural. These nouns are masculine.

     l'animal *animal* ➤ **les animaux** *animals*

     le cheval *horse* ➤ **les chevaux** *horses*

     l'hôpital *hospital* ➤ **les hôpitaux** *hospitals*

     le journal *newspaper* ➤ **les journaux** *newspapers*

     le travail *work* ➤ **les travaux** *works, construction work*

II. Agreement of Adjectives

■ Adjectives are words that describe a noun: *interesting, red, good, happy.* French adjectives agree with the noun they describe (or modify) in gender and number.

■ Adjectives ending in a consonant such as **intelligent** *(intelligent)* add **-e** to form the feminine and **-s** to form the plural.

	masculine	feminine
singular	intelligent	intelligente
plural	intelligents	intelligentes

■ The addition of **-e** shows that the final consonant (here **-t**) is pronounced in the feminine form; it is silent in the masculine. The plural ending **-s** is silent.

- Adjectives ending in **-e** such as **sympathique** *(nice, pleasant)* do not have a special form for the feminine, but add **-s** to form the plural. All forms sound alike.

	masculine	feminine
singular	sympathique	sympathique
plural	sympathiques	sympathiques

- Adjectives ending in **-i** or **-u** such as **poli** *(polite)* add **-e** to form the feminine and **-s** to form the plural, but all four forms sound alike.

	masculine	feminine
singular	poli	polie
plural	polis	polies

Note: An adjective that describes both a masculine and a feminine noun or a mixed group is masculine plural.

Le garçon et **la fille** sont **intelligents.** *The boy and the girl are intelligent.*

Pour décrire les copains

intelligent *intelligent*	**impoli** *impolite*
bête *silly, stupid*	**patient** *patient*
sympathique *nice, pleasant*	**impatient** *impatient*
pénible *annoying*	**timide** *shy*
poli *polite*	

Les amis et les copains

French people distinguish between **les amis** and **les copains. Les amis** are people whom you are very close to, like "best friends" in the U.S. **Un copain** or **une copine** is someone you are friendly with, but not necessarily your "best friend." **Les copains** refers to the group of friends a young person spends time with. French teenagers often go out in groups rather than on dates in pairs.

A. Mes camarades de classe. Françoise is describing the students in her class. Find out what she says about each one by creating sentences out of the strings of words. Make sure you make the adjectives agree.

Modèle Hélène/sympathique
➤ Hélène est sympathique.

1. Christine et Marc/poli

_____

2. Luc/timide

_____

3. Valérie et Jeanne/impatient

_____

4. Pierre et Philippe/bête

_____

5. Robert et Barbara/intelligent

_____

6. Monique/patient

_____

7. Antoine et Nicolas/pénible

_____

8. Annette/impoli

_____

B. Notre école. Olivier is describing his school to a French friend. Find out what he says about each part of the school by creating sentences out of the strings of words. Use two adjectives to describe each item, making both agree.

La description de l'école

large *wide*	**bas** *(fem. **basse**) low*
étroit *narrow*	**joli** *pretty*
long *(fem. **longue**) long*	**moderne** *modern*
court *short (not for people)*	**confortable** *comfortable*
grand *big*	**le bâtiment** *building*
petit *small, little*	**le couloir** *corridor*
haut *high, tall*	**le directeur/la directrice** *principal*

Modèle   l'école/grand/joli
  ➤ L'école est grande et jolie.

1. le bâtiment/haut/moderne

   _____

2. le terrain de sport/large/long

   _____

3. les couloirs/court/étroit

   _____

4. les salles de classe/petit/confortable

   _____

5. le bureau du directeur/petit/joli

   _____

6. les fenêtres/grand/haut

   _____

7. les tables/bas/long

   _____

8. la cantine/grand/moderne

   _____

III. Irregular Feminine Forms and Plurals

- Adjectives ending in **-x** change the **-x** to **-se** to form the feminine singular.

  merveilleu**x** ➤ merveilleu**se** *wonderful*

  ennuyeu**x** ➤ ennuyeu**se** *boring*

- Adjectives ending in **-s** or **-x** do not add an **-s** in the masculine plural.

	masculine	feminine
singular	merveilleux	merveilleuse
plural	merveilleux	merveilleuses

	masculine	feminine
singular	mauvais	mauvaise
plural	mauvais	mauvaises

- You have already seen the irregular feminine forms **longue** and **basse**.

- Many nouns that end in **-u** form their plural in **-x**.

  le jeu ➤ les jeux

  le bureau ➤ les bureaux

C. **Les passe-temps.** Ghislaine gives her opinion about things she does in her free time. Create sentences with **être** and the adjectives given to find out what she says. Pay close attention to the correct form of the adjective.

La description des activités

amusant *amusing, funny*	**formidable** *terrific*
difficile *hard, difficult*	**intéressant** *interesting*
embêtant *boring, annoying*	**merveilleux** *wonderful*
ennuyeux *boring*	**passionnant** *exciting*
facile *easy*	

Les loisirs

les bandes dessinées *(fem. pl.)* *comics, comic strips*	**le jeu vidéo** *video game*
	la revue *magazine*
les dessins animés *(masc. pl.)* *cartoons (TV), movies*	**le roman** *novel*
l'émission *(fem.)* *TV program*	**le roman d'aventures** *adventure novel*
le film *movie, film*	**la surboum** *party*

Modèle le roman/formidable

     ➤ Le roman est formidable.

1. le film/intéressant

    _____

2. les dessins animés/amusant

    _____

3. les bandes dessinées/merveilleux

    _____

4. les jeux vidéo de Claude/passionnant

    _____

5. l'émission/embêtant

    _____

6. le roman d'aventures en français/difficile

    _____

7. la surboum/ennuyeux

    _____

8. la revue/facile

    _____

IV. Position of Adjectives

■ Most French adjectives follow the noun they modify. This is the opposite of English usage where all adjectives precede their nouns.

Mme Dupré est **une femme intelligente.**	_Mrs. Dupré is **an intelligent woman.**_
Star Wars est **un film passionnant.**	_Star Wars is **an exciting film.**_

D. Je suis d'accord. Your friend is asking you about various friends at school. Agree with your friend's opinion about each one, by forming a sentence with the adjective following the nouns **garçon/garçons** or **fille/filles.**

Modèles —Jacques est intelligent, n'est-ce pas?
➢ —Oui, c'est un garçon intelligent.

—Jacques et Pierre sont intelligents, n'est-ce pas?
➢ —Oui, ce sont des garçons intelligents.

Les gens

charmant *charming*   paresseux *lazy*

doué *talented*   raisonnable *sensible*

généreux *generous*   sérieux *serious*

gentil *(fem.* gentille*)* kind, friendly   travailleur *(fem.* travailleuse*)*
                                   hard-working

heureux *happy*

malheureux *unhappy*

---

1. —Laurent est généreux, n'est-ce pas?

   — _____

2. —Michel et Rachelle sont paresseux, n'est-ce pas?

   — _____

3. —Anne est impatiente, n'est-ce pas?

   — _____

4. —Zoë et Charles sont charmants, n'est-ce pas?

   — _____

5. —Véronique est raisonnable, n'est-ce pas?

   — _____

6. —Les copines de Marc sont généreuses, n'est-ce pas?

   — _____

7. —Damien est travailleur, n'est-ce pas?

   — _____

8. —Virginie et Pauline sont douées, n'est-ce pas?

   — _____

E. Au contraire. A new student tells you things about fellow students that you don't agree with. Correct her using the phrase **au contraire.** Write out your exchanges with the new student, paying attention to the agreement and position of the adjectives.

Modèle   Georgette/bête/intelligent
—Georgette est bête, n'est-ce pas?
—Au contraire. Elle n'est pas bête. C'est une fille intelligente.

1. Christophe et Alain/pénible/sympathique

   — _____

   — _____

2. Marguerite/paresseux/travailleur

   — _____

   — _____

3. Bernard/charmant/embêtant

   — _____

   — _____

4. Suzanne et Danielle/poli/impoli

   — _____

   — _____

5. Catherine/impatient/patient

   — _____

   — _____

6. Thérèse et Françoise/malheureux/heureux

   — _____

   — _____

F. **Descriptions.** Create sentences out of each string of words that you can use to tell your friend what is going on. Make sure to put the adjectives in their correct position and to make them agree with the nouns they describe.

Modèle   nous/avoir/ une classe d'anglais/intéressant
    ➤ Nous avons une classe d'anglais intéressante.

1. Maric/organiser/une surboum/merveilleux

   _____

2. nous/regarder/des bandes dessinées/amusant

   _____

3. Guy et Marthe/étudier/un livre/facile

   _____

4. je/jouer à/des jeux vidéo/passionnant

   _____

5. nous/préparer/une leçon/difficile

   _____

6. Carole/écouter/des chansons/formidable

   _____

7. vous/avoir/des romans/intéressant

   _____

8. on/présenter/des émissions/merveilleux

   _____

G. **Composition.** Describe the following aspects of your world with a sentence beginning with **c'est.**

Modèle   your house
    ➤ C'est une maison moderne.

1. your school building   5. the novel you're reading

2. your French teacher   6. your favorite TV show

3. your best friend   7. your English class

4. the students in your school   8. a movie you want to see

Possessive and Demonstrative Adjectives; Adjectives that Come Before the Noun; Irregular Adjectives

I. Possessive Adjectives

■ Study the forms of the possessive adjectives in French.

singular:

	masculine	feminine	plural
first person	mon	ma	mes
second person	ton	ta	tes
third person	son	sa	ses

plural:

	masculine/feminine	plural
first person	notre	nos
second person	votre	vos
third person	leur	leurs

Notes:

1. Possessive adjectives in French agree in gender and number with the following noun.

mon livre	*my book*
ma calculatrice	*my calculator*
mes livres, **mes** calculatrices	*my books, my calculators*
ton livre	*your book*
ta calculatrice	*your calculator*
tes livres, **tes** calculatrices	*your books, your calculators*

2. The possessive adjectives **notre, votre,** and **leur** have the same form before masculine and feminine nouns: **leur calculatrice, leur livre.**

3. The possessive adjective **son/sa/ses** means *his, her, its.* Context clarifies the meaning.

Pierre est dans **sa** chambre.	*Pierre is in his room.*
Marie est dans **sa** chambre.	*Marie is in her room.*

4. If a feminine noun begins with a vowel or a mute **h, mon, ton,** and **son** replace **ma, ta,** and **sa.**

—J'aime bien **ton affiche.**	*I really like your poster.*
—**Mon affiche** de Paris?	*My poster of Paris?*
—Oui, l'affiche au mur, là, près de **ton étagère.**	*Yes, the poster on the wall there, near your bookcase.*

A. C'est à qui? Complete the following sentences with the possessive adjective corresponding to the subject to explain that the members of the class are ready to begin.

Modèle Vous avez _vos_ livres.

1. J'ai _____ crayon et _____ stylo.

2. Janine et Odile ont _____ classeurs.

3. Édouard a _____ disquette.

4. Monique a _____ cahier d'exercices.

5. Nous avons _____ cassette.

6. Le professeur a _____ carte de France.

7. Tu as _____ papiers.

8. Luc et Jean ont _____ magnétophone.

B. Ce n'est pas ça. Jean-Paul and Hélène are trying to figure out to whom things belong. Jean-Paul guesses the owner of each item but Hélène tells him it's not that person's.

Modèle —C'est le livre de Louise?
➤ —Non, ce n'est pas son livre.

1. —C'est l'imprimante de Simone?

   — _____

2. —Ce sont les crayons de Roger?

   — _____

3. —C'est l'ordinateur de Marc et de Philippe?

   — _____

4. —Ce sont les cahiers d'exercices des étudiants?

   — _____

5. —C'est la voiture du médecin?

   — _____

6. —C'est le chat d'Eugénie?

   — _____

➤➤➤➤➤➤

7. —Ce sont les disquettes de Julie et d'Élisabeth?

—_____

8. —Ce sont tes photos?

—_____

C. **Une famille sympathique.** Study this family tree to get to know the people. Then, tell what the people in the pictures are doing with which family member. Use the cues given to start your sentence. Each response should contain the preposition **avec,** a possessive adjective, and the word for the family member you see.

M. et Mme Pernod

Albert Durocher   Lucille Pernod   Jean-Luc Durocher   Suzanne Vernou

Janine   Maurice   Chantal   Robert

Modèle   Janine/étudier
➤ Janine étudie avec sa cousine.

1. Maurice/jouer aux cartes

   _____

   _____

2. Janine/regarder la télé

   _____

   _____

3. Maurice et Janine/entrer dans un magasin

   _____

   _____

4. Maurice et Janine/dîner

   _____

   _____

5. Albert Durocher/parler

   _____

   _____

6. Maurice et Janine/jouer au volley-ball

   _____

   _____

II. Demonstrative Adjectives

■ The English demonstrative adjectives are *this, that, these, those*. Study the following chart of the French demonstratives.

	masculine	feminine
singular	ce, cet	cette
plural	ces	ces

Notes:

1. If a masculine noun begins with a vowel or a mute **h**, **ce** changes to **cet**.

   ce livre   ***this, that*** book

   cet appareil-photo   ***this, that*** camera

2. The French demonstrative adjective means both *this* and *that*. The suffix **-ci** can be added to a noun to specify the meaning *this* or *these* and the suffix **-là** can be added to specify the meaning *that* or *those*.

   Frédéric aime **cette** voiture-**ci**,   *Frederick likes **this** car,*
   mais sa sœur aime **cette** voiture-**là**. *but his sister likes **that** car.*

D. Qu'est-ce que tu aimes? Chantal, a new student, is telling about all the things she likes in her new city. To find out what she says, complete these sentences with the correct demonstrative adjective.

1. J'aime _____ école.

2. J'aime _____ stade.

3. J'aime _____ maisons.

4. J'aime _____ aéroport.

5. J'aime _____ magasins.

6. J'aime _____ bibliothèque.

7. J'aime _____ piscine.

8. J'aime _____ théâtre.

E. Au magasin des appareils électroménagers (*At the home appliance store*). Imagine that you are shopping for appliances in France. Ask the clerk to show you various items using the phrase **Montrez-moi** (*Show me*) and a demonstrative. Don't forget to say please!

Modèle   le magnétophone
➤ Montrez-moi ce magnétophone, s'il vous plaît.

Les appareils électroménagers

le magnétophone *cassette player*   le répondeur *answering machine*

le magnétoscope *VCR*   le sèche-cheveux *hair dryer*

le rasoir électrique *electric shaver*

1. répondeurs

   _____

2. ordinateur

   _____

3. calculatrice

   _____

4. rasoirs électriques

   _____

5. sèche-cheveux

   _____

6. magnétoscope

   _____

7. appareil-photo

   _____

8. caméra

   _____

III. Irregular Adjectives

■ Adjectives that end in -s or -x in the masculine singular do not add another -s in the masculine plural. These adjectives have three forms. Remember that adjectives ending in -x change the -x to -se to form the feminine singular.

	masculine	feminine
singular	bas	basse
plural	bas	basses

	masculine	feminine
singular	mauvais	mauvaise
plural	mauvais	mauvaises

	masculine	feminine
singular	sérieux	sérieuse
plural	sérieux	sérieuses

■ Most adjectives that end in **-eur** have a feminine that ends in **-euse.**

travail**leur** ➤ travail**leuse**

■ Some adjectives have irregular feminine forms.

bas ➤ ba**sse**   long ➤ long**ue**

■ Adjectives that end in **-el, -en,** and **-on** double the final consonant of the masculine form before adding the feminine ending **-e.**

ACTUEL *PRESENT, PRESENT-DAY*

	masculine	feminine
singular	actuel	actue**lle**
plural	actuels	actue**lles**

CRUEL *CRUEL*

	masculine	feminine
singular	cruel	crue**lle**
plural	cruels	crue**lles**

BON *GOOD*

	masculine	feminine
singular	bon	bo**nne**
plural	bons	bo**nnes**

IV. Adjectives That Precede Their Nouns; Forms of *beau, nouveau, vieux*

■ Although most French adjectives follow their nouns, a small group of common adjectives precedes the noun.

beau *beautiful*

bon *(fem.* **bonne***) good*

gentil *(fem.* **gentille***) nice, kind, friendly*

grand *big, tall*

jeune *young*

joli *pretty*

long *(fem.* **longue***) long*

mauvais *bad*

nouveau *new*

petit *little, short*

vieux *old*

Nous avons une **petite voiture.**

*We have a **little car.***

Il y a un **joli jardin** derrière la maison.

*There's a **pretty garden** behind the house.*

Qui sont ces **jeunes gens?**

*Who are these **young men?***

■ The adjectives **beau, nouveau,** and **vieux** have irregular forms. They form their feminine in **-lle.** In addition, they have a special form ending in **-l** used before masculine singular nouns beginning with a vowel or a mute **h.**

	masculine	masculine before a vowel	feminine
singular	beau	bel	belle
plural	beaux		belles
singular	nouveau	nouvel	nouvelle
plural	nouveaux		nouvelles
singular	vieux	vieil	vieille
plural	vieux		vieilles

Notes:

1. The special forms used before masculine singular nouns are used only when the adjective (or the demonstrative) stands right before the noun.

   cet ordinateur *but* **ce nouvel** ordinateur

2. When an adjective comes before the noun, the plural definite article **des** usually changes to **de.**

   Nous avons **des livres** *but* Nous avons **de nouveaux livres.**

F. **Tout est nouveau.** Your city has many new things. Tell a friend what they are by completing the following sentences with the correct form of **nouveau.**

1. Il y a une _____ piscine.

2. Il y a un _____ stade.

3. Il y a de _____ jardins.

4. Il y a de _____ écoles.

5. Il y a un _____ aéroport.

6. Il y a un _____ parc.

7. Il y a de _____ cinémas.

8. Il y a une _____ librairie.

G. **Visite de la ville.** What's there to see in this very old city? Jeanne recommends some historic sites to a foreign visitor using the phrase **il faut visiter** *(you must visit)*. Complete her sentences with the correct form of **vieux.**

Dans la ville

la **gare** *railway station*

l'**hôtel** *(masc.)* hotel

l'**immeuble** *(masc.) apartment house*

le **monument** *monument*

le **palais** *palace*

le **quartier** *neighborhood*

la **ruine** *ruin*

l'**université** *(fem.) university*

---

1. Il faut visiter ces _____ quartiers.

2. Il faut visiter ces _____ ruines.

3. Il faut visiter ce _____ monument.

4. Il faut visiter ce _____ hôtel.

5. Il faut visiter la _____ gare.

6. Il faut visiter le _____ palais.

7. Il faut visiter ce _____ immeuble.

8. Il faut visiter la _____ université.

Les hôtels et les quartiers

- The word **hôtel** in French means hotel, but it also means a luxurious city residence. Paris has many of these private **hôtels,** once the homes of the nobility, especially in the area of the right bank of the Seine called **Le Marais.**
- The word **quartier** is not only the French term for neighborhood, but also an administrative term in Paris. Paris is divided into 20 **arrondissements,** each with an administrative office called **une mairie.** Each **arrondissement** is in turn divided into 4 **quartiers.**

H. Tu visites la ville. You're visiting a French city with a French friend. As you are shown around you comment how beautiful everything is. Write out what you would say at each place using **c'est** or **ce sont** and the correct form of **beau.** Remember that **des** changes to **de** when an adjective precedes the noun.

Modèle   quartier
      ➤ C'est un beau quartier.

1. aéroport   _____

2. parcs   _____

3. librairies   _____

4. bibliothèque   _____

5. hôtel   _____

6. monuments   _____

7. théâtre   _____

8. immeuble   _____

V. More than One Adjective

- When you want to use two adjectives to describe a noun, each one goes in its usual position.

une **grande** maison **moderne**	*a **big, modern** house*
un **beau** garçon **charmant**	*a **handsome, charming** boy*

- When both adjectives usually precede or usually follow the noun, they are joined by **et.**

un **grand et joli** jardin	*a **big, pretty** garden*
une femme **intelligente et travailleuse**	*an **intelligent, hard-working** woman*

- Sometimes phrases such as **jeune homme, jeune femme, jeune garçon, jeune fille** are treated as if they were nouns, so when another adjective is added, **et** is not used.

une **grande jeune** fille	*a **tall** girl*
un **nouveau jeune** homme	*a **new young** man*

I. **La famille de Gilles.** Describe Gilles's family and some of the things they have by adding the adjectives to each sentence in their proper form and position. Remember that **des** changes to **de** before an adjective.

Modèle   Gilles a une mère. (charmant, sympathique)
  ➤ Gilles a une mère charmante et sympathique.

1. La famille de Gilles a un appartement. (vieux/confortable)

   _____

2. L'appartement a une cuisine. (grand/moderne)

   _____

3. Gilles a une sœur. (raisonnable/doué)

   _____

4. Le père de Gilles a une voiture. (noir, vieux)

   _____

5. Gilles a une chambre. (charmant, petit)

   _____

6. L'appartement a des fenêtres. (grand, beau)

   _____

7. Gilles a des jeux vidéo. (merveilleux, passionnant)

   _____

8. Gilles a un cousin. (gentil, intelligent)

   _____

J. **Pour passer le temps.** What are people doing in their free time? Create sentences out of the strings of elements given to describe their activities. Pay special attention to the position and agreement of the adjectives.

Modèle   nous/regarder/films/vieux/formidable
➤ Nous regardons de vieux films formidables.

1. Louise/raconter/histoire/long/merveilleux

    _____

2. Monique/chercher/roman/facile/intéressant

    _____

3. Claude et Paul/regarder/match/important/passionnant

    _____

4. je/écouter/chansons/beau/moderne

    _____

5. tu/avoir/jeux vidéo/nouveau/amusant

    _____

6. Marc et Barbara/préparer/déjeuner/grand/délicieux

    _____

7. vous/parler avec/étudiant/nouveau/sympathique

    _____

8. Catherine/trouver/photos/vieux/intéressant

    _____

K. **Composition.** Write five sentences about what you do in your free time or five sentences that describe your family and your house or apartment. Try to vary the verbs and use two adjectives in at least four of the five sentences.

-Ir Verbs; Stressed Pronouns

I. Verbs Ending in *-ir*

■ Study the endings of the verbs ending in -**ir**.

FINIR *TO FINISH*

singular		**plural**	
je	finis	nous	finissons
tu	finis	vous	finissez
il/elle	finit	ils/elles	finissent
on	finit		

Notes:

1. The plural forms of -**ir** verbs have -**iss**- inserted before the endings (**finissons, finissez, finissent**).

2. The singular forms (**finis, finis, finit**) all sound alike.

■ Some useful -**ir** verbs

applaudir *to applaud*	**maigrir** *to get thinner, lose weight*
choisir *to choose*	**réfléchir** *to think over, reflect*
finir *to finish*	**réussir** *to succeed, pass (a test, a course)*
grossir *to get fat*	**ne pas réussir** *to fail (a test, a course)*

A. Quels sujets? Check all the possible subjects each verb form corresponds to.

1. finissent

    je ___ tu ___ il ___ elle ___ on ___ nous ___ vous ___ ils ___ elles ___

2. réussis

    je ___ tu ___ il ___ elle ___ on ___ nous ___ vous ___ ils ___ elles ___

3. applaudit

    je ___ tu ___ il ___ elle ___ on ___ nous ___ vous ___ ils ___ elles ___

4. maigrissez

    je ___ tu ___ il ___ elle ___ on ___ nous ___ vous ___ ils ___ elles ___

5. réfléchit

    je ___ tu ___ il ___ elle ___ on ___ nous ___ vous ___ ils ___ elles ___

6. choisissent

je ___ tu ___ il ___ elle ___ on ___ nous ___ vous ___ ils ___ elles ___

7. grossit

je ___ tu ___ il ___ elle ___ on ___ nous ___ vous ___ ils ___ elles ___

8. finis

je ___ tu ___ il ___ elle ___ on ___ nous ___ vous ___ ils ___ elles ___

B. Qu'est qu'on choisit? Tell what each person is selecting for his or her free time by adding the correct form of the verb **choisir** to each of the following sentences.

1. Je _____ un roman d'aventures.

2. Ma sœur _____ un disque compact.

3. Nous _____ un film amusant.

4. Mes petits frères _____ des dessins animés.

5. Mon père _____ une revue.

6. Vous _____ un match de basket-ball.

7. Tu _____ un livre.

8. Mes grands-parents _____ une émission à la télé.

C. Les devoirs. Everyone is finishing his or her homework. Say so using the correct form of **finir** followed by the appropriate possessive adjective.

Modèle Serge
➤ Serge finit ses devoirs.

1. Odile et Lise _____

2. Vous _____

3. Tu _____

4. Luc _____

5. Je _____

6. Les étudiants _____

7. Nous _____

8. Alice _____

D. C'est pour ça. Your friend tells you who studies a lot. You answer in each case that that's why those students pass their exams. Use the phrase **c'est pour ça que** *(that's the reason why)* and the verb **réussir.**

Note: The word **que** *(that)* becomes **qu'** before a word beginning with a vowel. The dropping of a vowel before another vowel is called *elision.*

Modèle —Jean étudie beaucoup.
➤ —C'est pour ça qu'il réussit.

1. —Tu étudies beaucoup.

   —_____

2. —Cet étudiant étudie beaucoup.

   —_____

3. —Anne et Danielle étudient beaucoup.

   —_____

4. —J'étudie beaucoup.

   —_____

5. —Albert étudie beaucoup.

   —_____

6. —Mes amis étudient beaucoup.

   —_____

7. —Marie étudie beaucoup.

   —_____

8. —Nous étudions beaucoup.

   —_____

E. Mais non! Say that your friend's impressions are not true.

Modèle —Jacques finit aujourd'hui.
➤ —Mais non! Il ne finit pas aujourd'hui.

1. —Je grossis.

   —_____

2. —Les étudiants réfléchissent.

   —_____

3. —Le public applaudit.

   — _____

4. —Tes amis choisissent de bons films.

   — _____

5. —Paulette réussit toujours.

   — _____

6. —Vous finissez vos devoirs.

   — _____

7. —Nous grossissons.

   — _____

8. —Tu maigris.

   — _____

F. **Finir sans réfléchir.** Say in each case that people are finishing their
   work rather than thinking things over. Change the possessive adjective as
   necessary.

Modèle Françoise
   ➤ Françoise ne réfléchit pas. Elle finit son travail.

1. Ton oncle _____

2. Vous _____

3. On _____

4. Les copains _____

5. Tu _____

6. Je _____

7. Ma grand-mère _____

8. Nous _____

II. Stressed Pronouns

■ In addition to the subject pronouns that you have learned, French has a set of "stressed pronouns."

	singular	plural
first person	moi	nous
second person	toi	vous
third person	lui/elle	eux/elles

■ Stressed pronouns are used to contrast two subjects.

Toi, tu réussis, mais **moi,** je ne réussis pas.

*You are passing, but **I** am not passing.*

Elle, elle maigrit, mais **eux,** ils grossissent.

*She's getting thinner, but **they're** getting fatter.*

■ Stressed pronouns can be used by themselves to answer a question.

—Qui est prêt?
—**Moi.**

Who's ready?
I (am).

■ Stressed pronouns are used after prepositions.

Je parle **avec lui.**

*I speak **with him.***

Il parle **avec moi.**

*He speaks **with me.***

■ Stressed pronouns appear after **c'est** and **ce sont** to identify people. (**Ce sont** is used with **eux** and **elles** only.)

	singular	plural
first person	C'est moi.	C'est nous.
second person	C'est toi.	C'est vous.
third person	C'est lui. C'est elle.	Ce sont eux. Ce sont elles.*

Note: When a stressed pronoun precedes the corresponding subject pronoun, it is usually set off by a comma.

Moi, je parle anglais.
Toi, tu parles espagnol.

G. Qui finit? Use stressed pronouns to say who is finishing and who is not. Follow the model.

Modèle   il/tu
   ➢ Lui, il finit, mais toi, tu ne finis pas.

1. vous/je

_____

2. ils/elle

_____

_____
* In the negative you say **Ce n'est pas eux, ce n'est pas elles.**

3. nous/tu

_____

4. il/elles

_____

5. je/tu

_____

6. vous/nous

_____

7. tu/il

_____

8. elle/ils

_____

H. Et inversement *(And vice-versa).* Continue each of the following statements by saying the reverse is also true. Replace any names by the corresponding stressed pronoun.

Modèle   Moi, je parle avec Jean-Claude.
➤ Et lui, il parle avec moi.

1. Les enfants jouent avec leur mère.

_____

2. Élisabeth travaille à côté de moi.

_____

3. Les étudiants apportent des cadeaux pour leur professeur.

_____

4. Jacques danse avec Marie-Claire.

_____

5. Moi, je passe l'après-midi avec toi.

_____

6. Nous, nous jouons aux dames avec vous.

_____

I. **Conversation sur les cadeaux.** Write an exchange between a husband and wife as they discuss for whom they have bought these gifts.

Modèle calculatrice/Robert ➤
—La calculatrice est pour Robert?
—Oui, c'est pour lui.

1. affiche/Anne

   —_____

   —_____

2. chaîne-stéréo/toi

   —_____

   —_____

3. disque compact/nos cousins

   —_____

   —_____

4. caméra/Lise et Janine

   —_____

   —_____

5. poste de télé/ton père

   —_____

   —_____

6. livre/toi et moi

   —_____

   —_____

7. magnétoscope/l'oncle Jules et la tante Sophie

   —_____

   —_____

8. voiture/moi

—_____

—_____

The preposition *chez*

■ The preposition **chez** means *at the house of* or *in our (her, etc.) family.*
It often appears with stressed pronouns.

	singular	plural
first person	chez moi	chez nous
second person	chez toi	chez vous
third person	chez lui, chez elle	chez eux, chez elles

J. Chez nous. Respond in each case that things are happening not only with
these people but at their homes. Use the preposition **chez** and the stressed
pronoun in your responses.

Modèle   —Tu étudies avec Odile?
     ➤ —Oui, j'étudie chez elle.

1. —Michel travaille avec toi?

—_____

2. —Laurent joue aux échecs avec Luc et Pierre?

—_____

3. —Sylvie et Marthe, vous déjeunez avec ma sœur et moi?

—_____

4. —Il finit ses devoirs avec son copain?

—_____

5. —Nous passons l'après-midi avec vous?

—_____

6. —Tu dînes avec moi?

—_____

7. —Pierrette regarde un film avec ses copines?

—_____

8. —Tu écoutes des cassettes avec Mathieu?

—_____

K. Complétez! Add the necessary stressed pronouns to the following paragraph.

Je suis avec mes copains maintenant. Nous sommes chez Martine.

Le samedi nous sommes souvent chez _____ (1). Sa maison est très grande.

_____ (2), j'écoute des cassettes. Martine est avec Luc. Elle joue aux dames

avec _____ (3). Christine et François sont dans la cuisine. La mère de

Martine prépare le déjeuner avec _____ (4). Charles et Serge sont dans le

jardin. _____ (5), ils jouent toujours au football. La petite sœur de Martine

joue avec _____ (6). _____ (7), nous aimons beaucoup la maison de

Martine. Et _____ (8), où est-ce que vous passez vos samedis?

L. Composition. Write six sentences in which you contrast what you do
and what some of your friends do, or what you arc like and what your friends
are like. You can also contrast your friends with each other, or describe
members of your family. Remember to use stressed pronouns when
contrasting subject pronouns.

-*Re Verbs; Prendre; Uses of on*

I. Verbs Ending in -*re*

■ Study the conjugation of the -**re** verbs.

RENDRE *TO RETURN, GIVE BACK*

singular		**plural**	
je	rend**s**	nous	rend**ons**
tu	rend**s**	vous	rend**ez**
il/elle	rend	ils/elles	rend**ent**
on		rend	

■ Some useful -**re** verbs

attendre *to wait for*	**rendre** *to give back, to return*
descendre *to go downstairs*	**répondre** *to answer*
entendre *to hear*	**vendre** *to sell*
perdre *to lose*	

Notes:

1. The singular forms of -**re** verbs (**rends, rend**) all sound alike. The final -**d** of the stem is pronounced in the plural (**rendent**), but not in the singular (**rends**).

2. The verb **attendre**, like **chercher, écouter,** and **regarder,** is followed by a direct object (that is, there is no preposition).

J'attends mon amie Michèle.	*I'm waiting for my friend Michèle.*
Nous **attendons** l'autobus.	*We're waiting for the bus.*

3. The verb **répondre** is followed by the preposition **à.**

Les étudiants **répondent aux questions.**	*The students answer the questions.*
Le professeur **répond** à l'étudiant.	*The teacher answers the student.*

Les moyens de transport et les passagers

l'autobus *(masc.) city bus*	le passager/la passagère *passenger*
l'autocar *(masc.) intercity bus*	le TGV *high speed train*
l'avion *(masc.) airplane*	le/la touriste *tourist*
le bateau *boat*	le voyageur/la voyageuse *traveler*

A. Qu'est-ce qu'ils attendent? Tell what each of these people is waiting for. Use the verb **attendre** followed by a direct object.

Modèle   nos parents/train
    ➢ Nos parents attendent le train.

1. moi/un taxi _____

2. les étudiants/l'autobus _____

3. ce touriste/l'autocar _____

4. vous/le bateau _____

5. nous/le train _____

6. ces passagers/l'avion _____

7. toi/le métro _____

8. le voyageur/le TGV _____

Le transport

- The Paris **métro** is an efficient means of getting around the French capital. All parts of the city have subway stations, and transfers between lines are free. The first line of the Paris métro opened in 1900.
- The intercity **TGV** or **Train à Grande Vitesse** is a triumph of French technology. These trains run on special tracks and reach speeds of over 200 miles per hour. All major French cities are connected by the TGV.

B. Fournitures d'occasion *(Secondhand supplies).* It's the end of the school year and these college students are selling some of their books and supplies. Use the verb **vendre** and the appropriate possessive adjective to tell what each one is selling. Use stressed pronouns where indicated.

Modèle   Joséphine/dictionnaire
➤ Joséphine vend son dictionnaire.

1. Frédéric et Philippe/livres de classe

_____

2. Colette/calculatrice

_____

3. moi/cassettes de français

_____

4. Jean-Louis et toi/affiches

_____

5. toi/sac à dos

_____

6. Chantal et moi/cartes

_____

7. Justine/vieil ordinateur

_____

8. moi/vieille imprimante

_____

C. Dans la classe de français. Create sentences out of the strings of words to describe how Marguerite's French class begins today. Use stressed pronouns where indicated.

Modèle   les étudiants/descendre l'escalier
➢ Les étudiants descendent l'escalier.

1. nous/attendre le professeur

_____

2. moi/entendre le prof

_____

3. le professeur/entrer dans la salle de classe

_____

4. tout le monde/saluer le professeur

_____

5. le professeur/rendre les compositions

_____

6. moi/avoir une question

_____

7. le professeur/répondre à ma question

_____

8. après, nous/choisir un thème de conversation

_____

D. Les étourdis *(Forgetful people).* A group of friends is discussing the things they always lose. Use the verb **perdre,** the word **toujours** *(always),* and the appropriate possessive adjective to find out what they say. Use stressed pronouns when the subject is a pronoun.

Note: Adverbs such as **toujours** usually follow the verb directly in French.

Modèle   Alain/stylo
➢ Alain perd toujours son stylo.

l'agenda *(masc.) appointment book*	**le feutre** *felt-tipped pen*
le classeur *loose-leaf file*	**les lunettes** *(fem. pl.) eyeglasses*
la clé *key*	**le stylo à bille** *ballpoint pen*

1. Jeanne et Chantal/lunettes

   _____

2. le professeur/crayon

   _____

3. moi/agenda

   _____

4. toi/livre de classe

   _____

5. Luc/classeur

   _____

6. nous/cahiers

   _____

7. vous/ feutres

   _____

8. Josette/stylo à bille

   _____

II. *Prendre* and Verbs Like *prendre*

■ The verb **prendre** *(to take)* is irregular. Although it looks like an **-re** verb, it loses the **-d-** of the infinitive in the plural. The third-person plural is written with a double **-n-**.

singular		plural	
je	prends	nous	prenons
tu	prends	vous	prenez
il/elle/on	prend	ils/elles	prennent

■ The verbs **apprendre** *(to learn)* and **comprendre** *(to understand)* are conjugated like **prendre.**

APPRENDRE *TO LEARN*

singular		plural	
j'	apprends	nous	apprenons
tu	apprends	vous	apprenez
il/elle/on	apprend	ils/elles	appren**nn**ent

COMPRENDRE *TO UNDERSTAND*

singular		plural	
je	comprends	nous	comprenons
tu	comprends	vous	comprenez
il/elle/on	comprend	ils/elles	compren**nn**ent

E. Comment est-ce qu'on voyage? Everyone is traveling today. Use the verb **prendre** to tell how. Use stressed pronouns when the subject is a pronoun.

Modèle Annick/métro
➤ Annick prend le métro.

1. moi/avion _____

2. les avocats/un taxi _____

3. les étudiants/autobus _____

4. nous/le train _____

5. ce voyageur/TGV _____

6. toi/autocar _____

7. les touristes/bateau _____

8. vous/le métro _____

F. Pourquoi est-ce qu'on ne répond pas? Write exchanges with the verbs **répondre** and **comprendre** that explain that each of the following people isn't answering because he or she doesn't understand.

Note: The phrase **c'est que** introduces the reason or explanation for something. The conjunction **que** undergoes elision and is written **qu'** before the pronouns **il, elle, ils, elles, on** and before other words beginning with a vowel or a mute **h.**

Modèle Henri ➤
—Henri ne répond pas.
—C'est qu'il ne comprend pas.

1. ces étudiantes

   — _____

   — _____

2. tu

   — _____

   — _____

3. Sylvie

   — _____

   — _____

4. vous

   — _____

   — _____

5. ces jeunes garçons

   — _____

   — _____

6. je

   — _____

   — _____

7. nous

   — _____

   — _____

8. M. et Mme Durand

   — _____

   — _____

G. **Les affaires internationales.** These students are planning careers in international business. Use the verb **apprendre** to tell what language each one is learning. Use stressed pronouns when the subject is a pronoun.

Note: French uses the definite article before the names of languages except directly after the verb **parler** and the prepositions **en** and **de**. The names of languages are masculine, so the article is **le** (**l'** before a vowel).

Modèle   Chantal/français
          ➤ Chantal apprend le français.

1. vous/chinois   _____

2. Claudette et Marie/allemand   _____

3. moi/espagnol   _____

4. toi/italien   _____

5. Alain/anglais   _____

6. nous/portugais   _____

7. Guy et Michel/japonais   _____

8. toi et moi/russe   _____

III. Uses of the Pronoun *on*

■ The French subject pronoun **on** is a non-specific subject like *one* or *people* in English. It is used to express what is done in general. The pronoun **on** is always used with the third-person singular form of the verb.

On parle français à Québec.	*French **is spoken** in Quebec (city).*
On attend l'autobus ici.	*Here's where **you wait** for the bus.*
On vend des vêtements dans ce magasin.	*Clothing **is sold** in that store.*

■ There is no stressed pronoun for **on** as a non-specific subject. The possessives **son, sa, ses** are used with it.

■ In everyday French, **on** + the third-person singular of the verb is often used instead of **nous** to mean *we.*

—Comment est-ce que vous rentrez?	*How do you go home?*
—**On prend** l'autobus pour rentrer.	*We take the bus to go home.*
—Vous jouez au football cet après-midi?	*Are you playing soccer today?*
—Non, aujourd'hui **on étudie.**	*No, today **we're studying.***

■ **Nous** is used as the stressed pronoun for **on** when **on** means *we*. The possessive adjectives **notre** and **nos** can be used to mean *our* when **on** replaces **nous** as the subject of the sentence.

Nous, on n'a pas **nos** livres aujourd'hui.   *We don't have our books today.*

H. Des recommandations. Use the non-specific pronoun **on** to explain to a new student what is expected of people at your school.

Modèle   travailler beaucoup
               ➤ On travaille beaucoup.

1. ne pas parler en classe

_____

2. écouter le professeur

_____

3. apporter ses livres et ses cahiers

_____

4. arriver à l'heure

_____

5. finir ses devoirs

_____

6. être poli et patient

_____

7. ne pas perdre ses compositions

_____

8. ne pas jouer au morpion en cours *(class)*

_____

I. **Une journée typique.** Rewrite François's description of a typical day for him and his friends in everyday French by changing **nous** to **on.**

1. Nous arrivons à l'école.

_____

2. Nous parlons avec les copains.

_____

3. Nous entrons dans l'école.

_____

4. Nous avons des cours.

_____

5. Nous déjeunons à la cantine.

_____

6. Après les cours, nous jouons au basket-ball.

_____

7. Nous rentrons en autobus.

_____

8. Nous dînons à la maison avec nos parents.

_____

J. **Contrastes.** Hélène and Noëlle are not doing what Alain is doing. Write the exchanges between them to express that fact using the cues given. Use **on** instead of **nous** in Hélène and Noëlle's responses, and use stressed pronouns as in the model.

Modèle dîner au restaurant/dîner à la maison ➤
            ALAIN: Moi, je dîne au restaurant. Et vous?
      HÉLÈNE ET NOËLLE: Nous, on dîne à la maison.

1. prendre le métro/prendre un taxi

    ALAIN: _____

HÉLÈNE ET NOËLLE: _____

2. ne pas comprendre le professeur/comprendre le professeur

    ALAIN: _____

HÉLÈNE ET NOËLLE: _____

3. apprendre l'anglais/apprendre l'allemand

    ALAIN: _____

HÉLÈNE ET NOËLLE: _____

4. perdre toujours mes affaires/ne pas perdre nos affaires

    ALAIN: _____

HÉLÈNE ET NOËLLE: _____

5. vendre mon vélo/ne pas vendre nos vélos

    ALAIN: _____

HÉLÈNE ET NOËLLE: _____

6. ne pas réussir en maths/réussir en maths

    ALAIN: _____

HÉLÈNE ET NOËLLE: _____

7. rentrer en autobus/rentrer en voiture

    ALAIN: _____

HÉLÈNE ET NOËLLE: _____

8. finir mes devoirs aujourd'hui/finir nos devoirs demain

    ALAIN: _____

HÉLÈNE ET NOËLLE: _____

K. **Composition.** Write a paragraph of five or six sentences that tells how you or you and your friends get to school. Whom do you see when you get to school? Are you always early or late? When and where do you talk with your friends?

I. *Pouvoir, vouloir,* and *devoir*

■ Learn the forms of the irregular verbs **pouvoir** *(to be able to)*, **vouloir** *(to want)*, and **devoir** *(ought, should, have to)*.

POUVOIR *TO BE ABLE TO, CAN*

singular		plural	
je	peux	nous	pouvons
tu	peux	vous	pouvez
il/elle/on	peut	ils/elles	peuvent

VOULOIR *TO WANT*

singular		plural	
je	veux	nous	voulons
tu	veux	vous	voulez
il/elle/on	veut	ils/elles	veulent

DEVOIR *OUGHT, SHOULD, HAVE TO*

singular		plural	
je	dois	nous	devons
tu	dois	vous	devez
il/elle/on	doit	ils/elles	doivent

■ **Pouvoir, vouloir,** and **devoir** can be followed by an infinitive.

—Tu **veux écouter** des cassettes?

*Do you **want to listen** to cassettes?*

—Je **ne peux pas écouter** des cassettes. Je **dois étudier.**

*I **can't listen** to cassettes. I **have to study.***

A. Anniversaires. What do the members of the Gautier family want for their birthdays this year? Robert Gautier goes over the gift list. To find out what he says, form sentences with the verb **vouloir** and add the appropriate indefinite article (**un, une, des**).

Modèle   ma mère/sèche-cheveux
➤ Ma mère veut un sèche-cheveux.

1. mon père/nouvelle voiture

_____

2. mon frère/rasoir électrique

_____

3. moi/magnétoscope

_____

4. mon frère et moi/jeux vidéo

_____

5. nos cousins/appareil-photo

_____

6. toi/répondeur

_____

7. ma sœur et toi/disques compacts

_____

8. nos grands-parents/nouveau poste de télé

_____

B. On ne veut pas. Today nobody wants to do anything. Use the negative of **vouloir** to tell what these people don't want to do. When the person is indicated by a pronoun, use both the stressed pronoun and the subject pronoun.

Modèle   lui/descendre
    ➤ Lui, il ne veut pas descendre.

Note: To make a verb such as **vouloir** negative when it comes before an infinitive, place the word **ne** before the form of **vouloir** and the **pas** after the form of **vouloir** (not after the infinitive) as in Lui, il **ne** veut **pas** descendre.

1. toi/travailler à la bibliothèque

_____

2. Sophie/écouter des chansons

_____

3. nous/dîner au restaurant

_____

4. Bernard et Jacquot/choisir un cadeau pour leurs parents

_____

5. moi/prendre le métro

_____

6. Monique et Jules/apprendre le vocabulaire

_____

7. nos copains/regarder un film

_____

8. Louise et toi/jouer aux cartes

_____

C. On ne peut pas. Say that people want to do these things but can't.
Use a stressed pronoun followed by a subject pronoun where called for.

Modèle Paul/finir
  ➤ Paul veut finir ses devoirs, mais il ne peut pas.

1. nous/inviter les copains

_____

2. M. Morot/enseigner l'italien

_____

3. toi/dessiner

_____

4. Charles et Bertrand/gagner le match

_____

5. vous/rester ici

_____

6. Hélène/monter à son appartement

_____

7. mon frère et sœur/rentrer maintenant

_____

8. moi/habiter à la campagne

_____

D. Obligations. Answer each of the following questions by saying that these people are not doing certain things, but that they ought to. Use **devoir** plus the infinitive of the verb of the question. Stressed pronouns are not necessary in the responses.

Modèle —Mireille étudie?
➢ —Non, mais elle doit étudier.

1. —Chantal et Sylvie travaillent dur?

   — _____

2. —M. Fournier vend sa maison?

   — _____

3. —Tu apprends les verbes par cœur?

   — _____

4. —La mère de Jacques travaille?

   — _____

5. —Mme Bertin et vous, vous prenez un taxi?

   — _____

6. —Ces étudiants réussissent?

   — _____

7. —Nous avons notre cours maintenant?

   — _____

8. —Je maigris?

   — _____

II. *Aller* (to go)

■ Learn the forms of the irregular verb **aller** *(to go)*.

ALLER *TO GO*

singular		plural	
je	vais	nous	allons
tu	vas	vous	allez
il/elle/on	va	ils/elles	vont

■ **Aller** is often followed by the preposition **à**, so remember to make the contractions **à + le ➢ au** and **à + les ➢ aux.**

—Vous **allez au** cinéma? *Are you going to the movies?*
—Non, nous **allons au** stade. *No, we're going to the stadium.*

—Vous **allez** souvent **aux** matchs *Do you often go to the soccer games?*
de football?
—Oui, nous aimons les sports. *Yes, we like sports.*

■ When **aller** is used before an infinitive it expresses future time, like English *to be going to do something.*

—Qui **va gagner** le match? Notre *Who's going to win the game?*
équipe? *Our team?*
—Nous, on **va perdre.** Notre équipe *We're going to lose. Our team is not*
n'est pas très bonne. *very good.*

■ **Aller** is also used to talk about general health or physical well-being.

—Bonjour, Madame. **Comment** *Good morning, Madam. **How are***
allez-vous? ***you?***
—**Je vais très bien,** merci. Et toi, *I'm fine, thank you. And what about*
Cléo? **Tu vas bien,** j'espère. *you, Cléo? **You're well,** I hope.*

E. **Un peu partout** *(Just about everywhere).* This group of friends is going to be all over town (and even out of town) today. Tell where they are going using the verb **aller,** the preposition **à,** and the definite article. Use a stressed pronoun followed by a subject pronoun where called for.

Modèle   mon frère/bibliothèque
➢ Mon frère va à la bibliothèque.

1. nos copains/stade

_____

2. ma sœur/magasins de vêtements

_____

3. Josette et Geneviève/parc

_____

4. moi/terrain de sport

_____

5. toi/librairie

_____

6. Gérard/théâtre

_____

7. vous/campagne

_____

8. nous/piscine

_____

F. Questions. Your friend tells you where people want to go. You ask if they are going to those places. Your friend says that they can't go. Continue the conversations following the model.

Modèle —Vincent veut aller au cinéma.
     ➤ —Est-ce qu'il va au cinéma?
       —Non, il ne peut pas.

1. —Marguerite veut aller au laboratoire de langues.

  — _____

  — _____

2. —Jacques et Martin veulent aller au parc.

  — _____

  — _____

3. —Le professeur veut aller au musée.

  — _____

  — _____

4. —Moi, je veux aller à l'aéroport.

  — _____

  — _____

5. —Les avocats veulent aller à leurs bureaux.

  — _____

  — _____

➤➤➤➤➤

6. —Nous, on veut aller à la campagne.

—_____

—_____

7. —Les étudiants veulent aller à la cantine.

—_____

—_____

8. —Moi, je veux aller à la salle de réunion.

—_____

—_____

Les musées

■ The **Musée du Louvre,** located in Paris, is one of the world's great art museums. Its collections of ancient art (Egypt, Ancient Near East) and European art (including Leonardo da Vinci's *Mona Lisa*) attract millions of visitors every year.
■ The **Cité des Sciences et de l'Industrie** is an ultra-modern hands-on museum of science and technology located at La Villette in northeastern Paris. Its symbol is **La Géode,** a huge sphere over 100 feet in diameter.

G. Où aller? Read what people have to do or want to do. Write two sentences for each person, one telling where he or she ought to go (using **devoir**) and one telling where he or she is going.

Modèle   Gilbert doit chercher un livre. (la bibliothèque)
➤ Il doit aller à la bibliothèque.
➤ Il va à la bibliothèque.

1. Stéphane aime les matchs. (le stade)

_____

_____

2. Marcelle et Éloïse prennent l'avion aujourd'hui. (l'aéroport)

_____

_____

3. Suzanne ne veut pas dîner chez elle. (le restaurant)

_____

_____

4. Marc veut parler avec Cécile. Elle est programmeuse. (le bureau)

_____

_____

5. Je veux voir le nouveau film. (le cinéma)

_____

_____

6. Nous voulons prendre le train pour aller à la campagne. (la gare)

_____

_____

7. Hubert veut jouer au football avec ses copains. (le terrain de sport)

_____

_____

8. Ma sœur a besoin de nouveaux vêtements. (le magasin)

_____

_____

H. Examen final en français! What are these students going to do to prepare for the French final exam? Construct sentences with **aller** + *infinitive* to describe their activities. Don't use stressed pronouns.

Modèle   Paul/apprendre le vocabulaire
➤ Paul va apprendre le vocabulaire.

1. nous/travailler dur

_____

2. Marc/réviser la grammaire

_____

➤➤➤➤➤

3. je/chercher mes vieux cahiers

_____

4. vous/répondre aux questions

_____

5. Albert/étudier chez nous

_____

6. tu/apporter les cassettes

_____

7. Luc et Sylvie/recopier leurs notes

_____

8. nous/réussir

_____

I. **Composition.** Write a paragraph of five or six sentences in which you tell about your plans for the weekend. Tell what you want to do, what you can or cannot do, and what you are going to do. To put events in sequence, words like **après** *(after, afterwards)* and **ensuite** *(following that, then)* will be useful. You might want to start your paragraph with **ce week-end** *(this weekend)*.

Irregular -er Verbs

I. Verbs Like *manger* and *commencer*

- Verbs ending in **-ger** are regular except for a change of **-g-** to **-ge-** in the first-person plural (**nous**) form. Verbs ending in **-cer** are regular except for a change of **-c-** to **-ç-** in the first-person plural. Study the conjugations of **manger** and **commencer.**

MANGER *TO EAT*

singular		plural	
je	mange	nous	man**ge**ons
tu	manges	vous	mangez
il/elle/on	mange	ils/elles	mangent

COMMENCER *TO BEGIN*

singular		plural	
je	commence	nous	commen**ç**ons
tu	commences	vous	commencez
il/elle/on	commence	ils/elles	commencent

Note:

Commencer is followed by the preposition **à** before an infinitive.

Je commence à comprendre.	*I'm beginning to understand.*
Nous commençons à travailler.	*We're beginning to work.*

- Verbs ending in **-ger**

changer *to change*	**nager** *to swim*
corriger *to correct*	**partager** *to share*
déménager *to move (to a new house, etc.)*	**ranger** *to put away*
déranger *to bother, disturb*	**rédiger** *to draft, write*
manger *to eat*	**voyager** *to travel*

- Verbs ending in **-cer**

annoncer *to announce*	**prononcer** *to pronounce*
commencer *to begin*	**remplacer** *to replace*
effacer *to erase*	

A. La classe de français. Answer these questions about your French class in the **nous** form. You may answer affirmatively or negatively.

1. Est-ce que vous prononcez correctement?

   _____

2. Est-ce que vous corrigez vos examens en classe?

   _____

3. Est-ce que vous effacez les mots incorrects dans vos compositions?

   _____

4. Est-ce que vous dérangez vos camarades de classe?

   _____

5. Est-ce que vous rédigez des lettres en français?

   _____

6. Est-ce que vous mangez en classe?

   _____

7. Est-ce que vous rangez vos affaires *(belongings)* après la classe?

   _____

8. Est-ce que vous commencez à comprendre le français?

   _____

B. Les vacances. Sophie tells about her summer vacation plans. To find out what she and her family are going to do, complete the following paragraph with the correct forms of the verbs in parentheses.

Cet été tout le monde _____ (1. voyager). Ma famille et moi,

nous _____ (2. voyager) en voiture. Nous _____ (3. aller)

dans le Midi *(South of France)*. Nous _____ (4. vouloir) louer une

petite maison. Moi, je _____ (5. vouloir) une maison au bord de

la mer, parce que j'_____ (6. aimer) la plage, mais ma sœur

_____ (7. vouloir) louer une maison au bord d'un lac. De toute façon,

nous _____ (8. aller) pouvoir nager. Pendant les vacances nous

_____ (9. nager) tous les jours. Nous _____ (10. manger) souvent au bord de l'eau. Nous _____ (11. aimer) beaucoup les vacances, mais elles _____ (12. être) trop courtes!

Le Languedoc

This region of southern France, called officially **Le Languedoc-Roussillon,** is located along the Mediterranean coast from the Spanish border almost to the mouth of the Rhône River. The Languedoc is France's largest producer of wine, and contains several of France's most famous sites: the **pont du Gard,** a well-preserved roman aqueduct; the medieval walled city of **Carcassone,** the Roman amphitheater at **Nîmes.** The regional capital is **Montpellier** and some other important cities of the region are **Perpignan, Narbonne, Arles,** and **Sète.**

II. Verbs Ending in *-yer*

■ Verbs ending in **-ayer, -oyer,** and **-uyer** such as **payer** *(to pay)*, **nettoyer** *(to clean)*, and **ennuyer** *(to bore)*, change the **-y-** to **-i-** before a silent **e.** In other words, all the singular forms and the third-person plural are spelled with **-i-** instead of **-y-.** Study the conjugations of **payer, nettoyer,** and **ennuyer.**

PAYER *TO PAY*

singular		plural	
je	paie	nous	payons
tu	paies	vous	payez
il/elle/on	paie	ils/elles	paient

NETTOYER *TO CLEAN*

singular		plural	
je	nettoie	nous	nettoyons
tu	nettoies	vous	nettoyez
il/elle/on	nettoie	ils/elles	nettoient

ENNUYER *TO BORE*

singular		plural	
j'	ennuie	nous	ennuyons
tu	ennuies	vous	ennuyez
il/elle/on	ennuie	ils/elles	ennuient

■ Verbs ending in **-yer**

appuyer *to press*

appuyer sur le bouton *to press the button*

appuyer sur une touche *to press a key (computer)*

employer *to use*

ennuyer *to bore*

envoyer *to send*

essayer *to try, try on*

essayer + **de** + infinitive *to try to do something*

payer *to pay*

tutoyer *to use the **tu** form to address someone*

vouvoyer *to use the **vous** form to address someone*

C. Moi aussi. Your friends tell you about what they are doing. You say that you are doing the same things. Make all necessary changes.

Modèle —Nous envoyons une lettre.
➢ —Moi aussi, j'envoie une lettre.

1. —Nous appuyons sur les touches de l'ordinateur.

— ____ _____

2. —Nous essayons de réussir.

— _____

3. —Nous nettoyons notre chambre.

— _____

4. —Nous tutoyons nos copains.

— _____

5. —Nous vouvoyons le directeur du collège.

— _____

6. —Nous employons une calculatrice.

— _____

7. —Nous payons pour aller au cinéma.

— _____

8. —Nous envoyons des cadeaux à nos amis.

— _____

D. Entre amis. The sentences below are all directed to M. Pascal. Redirect them to your friend Olivier. Change **nous** to **on** to make the tone more familiar, making sure to change the verb form accordingly.

Modèle   Nous payons trop, Monsieur Pascal.
        ➤ On paie trop, Olivier.

1. Est-ce que nous ennuyons les voisins, Monsieur Pascal?

    _____

2. Nous n'employons pas de dictionnaire, Monsieur Pascal.

    _____

3. Nous ne vouvoyons pas nos parents, Monsieur Pascal.

    _____

4. Nous tutoyons nos chats et nos chiens, Monsieur Pascal.

    _____

5. Combien est-ce que nous payons pour voir le match, Monsieur Pascal?

    _____

6. Quand est-ce que nous appuyons sur cette touche, Monsieur Pascal?

    _____

7. Qu'est-ce que nous envoyons à nos amis, Monsieur Pascal?

    _____

8. Quand est-ce que nous nettoyons notre chambre, Monsieur Pascal?

    _____

III. Other Changes Before Mute *-e*

■   The verb **acheter** changes the -e- of the stem to -è- before an ending containing a silent -e.

ACHETER *TO BUY*

singular		plural	
j'	achète	nous	achetons
tu	achètes	vous	achetez
il/elle/on	achète	ils/elles	achètent

- The verb **appeler** doubles the -l- before an ending containing a silent -e.

APPELER *TO CALL*

singular		plural	
j'	appelle	nous	appelons
tu	appelles	vous	appelez
il/elle/on	appelle	ils/elles	appellent

- The verb **jeter** doubles the -t- before an ending containing a silent -e.

JETER *TO THROW*

singular		plural	
je	jette	nous	jetons
tu	jettes	vous	jetez
il/elle/on	jette	ils/elles	jettent

- The verb **préférer** changes the -é- of the stem (the -é- in the syllable -fé-) to -è- before an ending containing a silent -e.

PRÉFÉRER *TO PREFER*

singular		plural	
je	préfère	nous	préférons
tu	préfères	vous	préférez
il/elle/on	préfère	ils/elles	préfèrent

- The verbs **célébrer** and **répéter** are conjugated like **préférer**. In both cases it is the second -é- that changes to -è-: **je célèbre, je répète.**

E. **Les matières.** What school subjects do these students like and which do they prefer? Use the expression **aimer bien** *(to like a lot)* and the verb **préférer.** Pay special attention to the change from -é- to -è-.

Modèle   vous/les maths/l'histoire
➤ Vous aimez bien les maths, mais vous préférez l'histoire.

1. je/les sciences/la géographie

   _____

2. Marthe et Solange/la géométrie/l'algèbre

   _____

3. Maurice/les langues/les sciences

   _____

4. Alexandre et Paul/la géographie/l'histoire

   _____

5. tu/la biologie/la chimie

_____

6. nous/la philosophie/la littérature

_____

7. vous/le français/le latin

_____

8. Carole/l'éducation civique/l'éducation physique

_____

Les matières

Secondary education in France includes subjects such as civics, philosophy, and geography. Some subjects have slang designations, such as **la géo** for **la géographie** and **la philo** for **la philosophie.** French secondary school students have Wednesdays off, but attend classes on Saturday morning.

F. **Au téléphone.** These people stay in touch by telephone. Use the verb **appeler** and the correct possessive adjective to say that these students call their friends.

Modèle Françoise
➤ Françoise appelle ses amis.

1. je _____

2. Monique et Marianne _____

3. Luc _____

4. tu _____

5. vous _____

6. Georges et Laurent _____

7. nous _____

8. ma sœur _____

G. Fournitures scolaires *(School supplies).* It's September and people are shopping for school supplies. Tell what the students are buying using the verb **acheter.** Use stressed pronouns followed by a subject pronoun where called for.

Modèle   Micheline/cahiers
➤ Micheline achète des cahiers.

1. Joseph/crayons _____

2. moi/calculatrice _____

3. Chantal/disquettes _____

4. Luc et son frère/ordinateur _____

5. nous/stylos _____

6. vous/feutres _____

7. Hélène et Christine/classeurs _____

8. toi/sac à dos _____

H. Pour une salle de classe ordonnée *(To have a neat classroom).* Use the verb **jeter** and the correct possessive adjective to say that these students keep the classroom neat by throwing their discarded papers in the wastebasket (**la corbeille**). Use stressed pronouns followed by a subject pronoun where called for.

Modèle   Dominique
➤ Dominique jette ses papiers à la corbeille.

1. Henri et Martin _____

2. toi _____

3. Cécile et Georgette _____

4. Philippe _____

5. moi _____

6. vous _____

7. nous _____

8. Sylvie _____

Voir, croire, dire, lire, écrire, venir

I. *Voir* and *croire*

■ The irregular verbs **voir** and **croire** are conjugated similarly.

VOIR *TO SEE*

singular		plural	
je	vois	nous	voyons
tu	vois	vous	voyez
il/elle/on	voit	ils/elles	voient

CROIRE *TO BELIEVE, TO THINK*

singular		plural	
je	crois	nous	croyons
tu	crois	vous	croyez
il/elle/on	croit	ils/elles	croient

■ The verb **voir** can be followed by noun objects as well as by subordinate (dependent) clauses.

Noun object

Je vois **le cinéma.**   *I see **the movie theater.***

Subordinate clause as object

Je vois **qu'il est fermé.**   *I see **that it is closed.***

■ The verb **croire** is most often followed by a subordinate clause.

Je crois **qu'il y a une séance ce soir.**   *I think **there's a showing (of the film) this evening.***

■ Some expressions with **voir** and **croire**

Je crois que oui.	*I think so.*
Je crois que non.	*I don't think so.*
C'est un film à voir.	*It's a film worth seeing.*
Voir la vie en rose.	*To take a rosy view of things.*
Voir la vie en noir.	*To take a negative view of things.*

A. Il faut vérifier *(We've got to check).* Here are some things people think are happening at school. Use the verb **croire** followed by a subordinate clause beginning with **que** to explain what they are. Use stressed pronouns where necessary.

Modèle Michel/nous avons beaucoup de devoirs pour demain
➤ Michel croit que nous avons beaucoup de devoirs pour demain.

1. Lucille et Robert/le professeur de biologie n'est pas là aujourd'hui

_____

2. toi/il y a un examen demain

_____

3. Pierre/il n'y a plus de gâteau à la cantine

_____

4. nous/il va pleuvoir cet après-midi

_____

5. le professeur de littérature/nous ne travaillons pas assez

_____

6. moi/il y a des activités parascolaires après les classes

_____

7. vous/nous n'apprenons pas beaucoup dans la classe d'anglais

_____

8. Laurent et Cécile/nous devons aller à la bibliothèque

_____

B. Les optimistes et les pessimistes. Use the expressions **voir la vie en rose** and **voir la vie en noir** to expand these statements. Don't use stressed pronouns in your responses.

Modèle Jacqueline est pessimiste.
➤ Elle voit la vie en noir.

1. Marc est optimiste. _____

2. Moi, je suis pessimiste. _____

3. Chantal et Danielle sont optimistes. _____

4. Christine est pessimiste. _____

5. Toi, tu es optimiste. _____

6. Nous, nous sommes pessimistes. _____

7. Jean et Philippe sont optimistes. _____

8. Vous, vous êtes pessimistes. _____

II. *Dire*

■ The verb **dire** *(to say, to tell)* is irregular.

DIRE *TO SAY, TO TELL*

singular		plural	
je	dis	nous	disons
tu	dis	vous	dites
il/elle/on	dit	ils/elles	disent

■ **Dire** can be followed by a noun object or by a subordinate clause.

Je dis **la vérité.**	*I'm telling **the truth.***
Il dit **qu'il est médecin.**	*He says **that he's a doctor.***

C. **Qu'est-ce qu'on dit?** Use the verb **dire** to specify what each person is saying or telling. Use stressed pronouns where necessary.

Qu'est-ce qu'on dit?

la bêtise *foolish thing*	**la réponse** *answer*
le mensonge *lie*	**la vérité** *truth*

Modèle Françoise/la vérité
➤ Françoise dit la vérité.

1. toi/des choses intelligentes

_____

2. le professeur/des choses importantes

_____

3. Lucille/des bêtises

_____

➤➤➤➤➤

4. Marc et Luc/des mensonges

_____

5. vous/«bonjour»

_____

6. moi/la réponse

_____

7. Marc et toi /beaucoup de choses

_____

8. nous/«au revoir»

_____

D. On dit que... People are discussing Jean's vacation. Turn each of their quotes into a subordinate clause by adding the appropriate form of the verb **dire** and the conjunction **que.**

Modèle   Suzanne: «Jean part en vacances.»
➤ Suzanne dit que Jean part en vacances.

1. Antoine: «Jean part lundi.»

_____

2. Moi: «Il part à huit heures.»

_____

3. Jean-Luc: «Il part en voiture.»

_____

4. Rachel et Jeanne: «Il a trois valises.»

_____

5. Toi: «Il va à Paris.»

_____

6. Philippe et Marie: «Il a beaucoup d'amis à Paris.»

_____

7. Vous: «Il va passer deux semaines à Paris.»

_____

8. Nous: «Il va rentrer le 15.»

_____

III. _Lire_ and _écrire_

■ Study the conjugations of the irregular verbs **lire** and **écrire.**

LIRE _TO READ_

singular		**plural**	
je	lis	nous	lisons
tu	lis	vous	lisez
il/elle/on	lit	ils/elles	lisent

ÉCRIRE _TO WRITE_

singular		**plural**	
j'	écris	nous	écrivons
tu	écris	vous	écrivez
il/elle/on	écrit	ils/elles	écrivent

E. Il y a beacoup à lire. Tell what each person is reading using the verb **lire.** Don't use stressed pronouns in this exercise.

Modèle Daniel/un livre
    ➤ Daniel lit un livre.

1. nous/les bandes dessinées

_____

2. le professeur/un livre de grammaire

_____

3. je/un roman

_____

4. les étudiants/des journaux français

_____

5. vous/une revue canadienne

_____

➤➤➤➤➤

6. les secrétaires/les dossiers

   _____

7. tu/une lettre de ta cousine

   _____

8. Paul/mes notes d'histoire

   _____

F. On écrit beaucoup. A friend says students read a lot in English class. You respond that they write a lot too. Fill in the missing forms of **lire** and respond using **écrire** as in the model.

Modèle —Jean _lit_ beaucoup dans la classe d'anglais.
➤ Oui, et il écrit beaucoup aussi.

1. —Tu _____ beaucoup dans la classe d'anglais.

   — _____

2. —Les étudiants _____ beaucoup dans la classe d'anglais.

   — _____

3. —Ton amie Marguerite _____ beaucoup dans la classe d'anglais.

   — _____

4. —Je _____ beaucoup dans la classe d'anglais.

   — _____

5. —Mes amis et moi, nous _____ beaucoup dans la classe d'anglais.

   — _____

6. —Tes copains et toi, vous _____ beaucoup dans la classe d'anglais.

   — _____

7. —Maurice et Jacques _____ beaucoup dans la classe d'anglais.

   — _____

8. —Nathalie et Sylvie _____ beaucoup dans la classe d'anglais.

   — _____

G. Qu'est-ce qu'on écrit? The students are all busy in study hall. Tell what each is writing using the appropriate form of the verb **écrire.** Use stressed pronouns where indicated.

Modèle   Chantal/un exercice
      ➤ Chantal écrit un exercice.

1. toi/tes devoirs

   _____

2. Gérard et Philippe/un problème de maths

   _____

3. Sophie/une composition

   _____

4. moi/une lettre

   _____

5. Jean-Pierre et toi/des réponses

   _____

6. nous/les verbes irréguliers

   _____

7. Corinne et Diane/des mots français

   _____

8. Olivier/une histoire

   _____

IV. *Venir*

■ Study the conjugation of the irregular verb **venir** *(to come).*

VENIR *TO COME*

singular		plural	
je	viens	nous	venons
tu	viens	vous	venez
il/elle/on	vient	ils/elles	viennent

■ The verb **revenir** *(to come back)* is conjugated like **venir: je reviens, tu reviens, il revient,** etc.

H. Les Canadiens. All the people asked about are Canadians. Write an exchange using the verb **venir** and the city that they come from. Don't use stressed pronouns.

Modèle   Rozianne/Montréal ➢
           —Rozianne est canadienne?
           —Oui, elle vient de Montréal.

1. Mathieu/Québec

    — _____

    — _____

2. Robert et Sylvie/Chicoutimi

    — _____

    — _____

3. tu/Trois-Rivières

    — _____

    — _____

4. vous *(pl.)*/Toronto

    — _____

    — _____

Le Canada

- **Canada** became a French colony in 1534 when **Jacques Cartier** explored the St. Lawrence River and took possession of Canada for France.
- **Samuel de Champlain** founded the city of Quebec in 1608. Montreal was founded in 1634.
- During the French and Indian War (**La Guerre de Sept Ans**), the British expelled to other British colonies the French-speaking residents of **Acadie** (today Nova Scotia) who refused to swear loyalty to the British Crown. Those deported to Louisiana (still a French colony at the time) became the Cajuns. The word *cajun* derives from **acadien.**
- The Treaty of Paris of 1763 awarded **La Nouvelle France** to Great Britain, and Canada became an English colony.
- Today, French is the native language of over a fourth of Canadians (over 6,000,000 people) and is the official language of the province of Quebec.

I. La boum! Sylvie and Joséphine are discussing who is coming to the party and who is not. Write an exchange between the two girls about each of the people mentioned. The words **oui** and **non** tell you whether or not the person asked about will come to the party. Use stressed pronouns where indicated.

Modèle   Philippe/oui ➤
   —Philippe vient à la boum?
   —Oui, il vient.

1. toi/oui

   —_____

   —_____

2. Rachel et Lucie/non

   —_____

   —_____

3. Luc/oui

   —_____

   —_____

4. moi/oui

   —_____

   —_____

5. tes cousins/non

   —_____

   —_____

6. Marc et toi/oui

   —_____

   —_____

➤➤➤➤➤

7. Laurent et moi/oui

— _____

— _____

8. Annette/non

— _____

— _____

J. **Avant la classe.** A group of students are chatting while waiting for their teacher. Complete their conversation by adding the correct forms of the verbs in parentheses.

MARC: Le professeur est en retard. Pourquoi est-ce qu'il ne _____ (1. venir) pas?

SERGE: Les professeurs _____ (2. venir) toujours à l'heure. Tu _____ (3. croire) qu'il est malade?

CÉCILE: Je _____ (4. croire) que non. On _____ (5. dire) qu'il y a une réunion des professeurs aujourd'hui.

CHANTAL: Eh, vous, là, Joseph et David, qu'est-ce que vous _____ (6. écrire)?

DAVID: Nous _____ (7. écrire) nos compositions.

ANNE: Et moi, je _____ (8. lire) le chapitre trois du livre. Pourquoi est-ce que vous ne _____ (9. lire) rien?

LUC: On préfère parler un peu. Écoute, Jacques, toi, tu es près de la porte. Si tu _____ (10. voir) le professeur, tu _____ (11. dire) quelque chose.

JACQUES: Je _____ (12. croire) qu'il vient. Oui, je _____ (13. voir) notre professeur. (*Tout le monde commence à étudier.*) Il _____ (14. revenir)!

LE PROF: Quand je _____ (15. revenir), je _____ (16. voir) que tout le monde travaille pendant mon absence. Vous _____ (17. lire) et vous _____ (18. écrire). Quels bons élèves!

V. Verbs of Motion with the Infinitive

- Verbs expressing motion such as **venir, descendre, monter, sortir, entrer, rentrer, revenir,** etc. can be followed directly by an infinitive. The infinitive tells the purpose for which people are coming or going.

—Tu **descends faire** les courses?

Are you going down to do the shopping?

—Oui, je **sors acheter** du pain et du lait.

Yes, I'm going out to buy bread and milk.

—Vous **venez dîner** chez nous?

Will you come (to) have dinner with us?

—Oui, on **vient manger** chez vous demain, si ça va.

Yes, we'll come eat at your place tomorrow if that's all right.

- Remember that the verb **aller** when followed by an infinitive refers to the future.

—Qu'est-ce que vous **allez lire** dans le train?

What are you going to read on the train?

—Nous **allons acheter** des revues.

We're going to buy magazines.

K. Les invités arrivent! The Mallet family has invited many people for dinner. Everyone is bustling about getting ready. Tell what each member of the family is doing to help by expanding each sentence with the verb of motion in parentheses.

Modèle Les invités arrivent. (aller)
> ➤ Les invités vont arriver.

1. Mme Mallet prépare le dîner. (aller)

   _____

2. M. Mallet achète de l'eau minérale. (sortir)

   _____

3. Joseph aide sa mère. (venir)

   _____

4. Sandrine cherche la belle nappe *(tablecloth)* blanche. (monter)

   _____

5. Moi, j'achète des bonbons. (descendre)

   _____

L. Composition. Write about the films you see, the books you read, and the things you write. Use verbs such as **croire** and **dire** to tell what you and others think about those things. Compose a paragraph of five or six sentences.

Direct Object Pronouns; Imperative

I. Direct Object Nouns

■ A direct object noun is one that answers the question *what* in relation to the verb. For instance, in the sentence *Michèle is reading the book, the book* is the direct object. It answers the question *What is Michèle reading?* Michèle is the subject of the sentence. The subject of the sentence determines the form of the verb in English and French.

■ Nouns referring to people and places can also be direct objects of a verb.

Jean **voit ses grands-parents** le dimanche.	*John sees his grandparents on Sundays.*
Nous **aimons Paris.**	*We love Paris.*

In the above sentences, **grands-parents** is the direct object of **voit** (answers the question **Qui est-ce que Jean voit?**) and **Paris** is the direct object of **aimons.**

II. Direct Object Pronouns—First and Second Persons

■ Study the direct object pronouns for the first and second persons.

	singular	plural
first person	me	nous
second person	te	vous

—On va prendre un café. Je **t'**invite.	*We'll go have a cup of coffee. It's my treat. (I'm inviting **you**.)*
—Tu **m'**invites? C'est très gentil.	*You're treating **me**? That's very nice.*
—Où est-ce que tu **nous** attends?	*Where are you waiting for **us**?*
—Je **vous** attends devant le cinéma.	*I'll wait for **you** (pl.) in front of the movies.*

■ The negative word **ne** precedes the object pronoun.

Tu **ne m'**invites **jamais**!	*You **never** invite **me**!*

■ Note that the direct object pronouns precede the conjugated verb in French. They follow it in English.

■ The pronouns **me** and **te** become **m'** and **t'** before a vowel or a mute **h.**

■ In verb + *infinitive* constructions, the direct object pronouns go between the conjugated verb and the infinitive.

—Quand est-ce que je **peux vous aider?**   *When **can** I **help** you?*

—Vous **pouvez venir me voir** à trois heures.   *You **can come** see me at three o'clock.*

In verb + *infinitive* constructions, the negative is formed around the conjugated verb. The object pronoun follows the negative word **pas, jamais, plus,** etc.

—Je **ne** veux **pas** vous déranger.   *I **don't** want to bother you.*

—Vous **n'**allez **pas** me déranger.   *You're **not** going to bother me.*

A. Les questions d'un(e) ami(e). Answer your friend's questions using the direct object pronoun **te (t').**

Quelques nouveaux verbes

accompagner *to accompany, go with*

admirer *to admire*

raccompagner *to walk (someone) home*

Modèles   —Tu m'aimes? (oui)
➤ —Oui, je t'aime.

—Tu m'aimes? (non)
➤ —Non, je ne t'aime pas.

1. —Tu m'accompagnes? (oui)   _____

2. —Tu m'entends? (non)   _____

3. —Tu m'admires? (oui)   _____

4. —Tu me cherches? (non)   _____

5. —Tu me comprends? (non)   _____

6. —Tu m'aides? (oui)   _____

7. —Tu me raccompagnes? (oui)   _____

8. —Tu m'attends? (non)   _____

B. Jean-Claude et toi. Suzanne is asking her friend Mireille about her relationship with Jean-Claude. Things don't seem to be going too well. Write Mireille's answers to Suzanne's questions.

Modèle   —Il t'aide? (non-jamais)
➤ —Non, il ne m'aide jamais.

1. —Il te raccompagne? (non-jamais)

    — _____

2. —Il t'écoute? (non-jamais)

    — _____

3. —Il t'invite? (non-jamais)

    — _____

4. —Il t'ennuie? (oui-beaucoup)

    — _____

5. —Il te comprend? (non-jamais)

    — _____

6. —Il te dérange? (oui-beaucoup)

    — _____

C. Les copains. Serge and Jean are asking Martin and Louis if they can do certain things. Martin and Louis answer with a verb + *infinitive* construction using the verb in parentheses and the direct object pronoun **vous.**

Modèle   —Vous nous attendez? (non-pouvoir)
➤ —Non, nous ne pouvons pas vous attendre.

1. —Vous nous accompagnez? (oui-aller)

    — _____

2. —Vous nous aidez? (non-pouvoir)

    — _____

3. —Vous nous entendez? (non-pouvoir)

    — _____

4. —Vous nous invitez? (oui-vouloir)

    — _____

5. —Vous nous voyez? (oui-venir)

   — _____

6. —Vous nous comprenez? (non-pouvoir)

   — _____

7. —Vous nous écoutez? (oui-aller)

   — _____

III. Direct Object Pronouns—Third-person Singular and Plural

■ Study the direct object pronouns for the third person.

singular	plural
le, la	les
l' *before a vowel*	

■ The third-person pronouns refer to both people and things. **Le** replaces any masculine singular noun, so **le** may mean *him* or *it*. **La** replaces any feminine singular noun and thus means *her* or *it*.

—Voilà Marguerite Leloup.   *There's Marguerite Leloup.*
—Où? Je ne **la** vois pas.   *Where? I don't see **her**.*

—La gare routière est au coin, là.   *The bus station is on the corner, there.*
—Où? Je ne **la** vois pas.   *Where? I don't see **it**.*

D. Un étudiant en difficulté. Mme Dulac is discussing her son Marc's problems at school with her friend Mme Delavigne. Mme Delavigne warns her that if Marc doesn't do what he's supposed to, he'll fail. Replace the direct object noun with a pronoun in writing Mme Delavigne's responses to her friend's concerns.

Modèle   —Marc n'écrit pas la composition.
     ➤ —S'il ne l'écrit pas, il ne va pas réussir.

1. —Marc n'écoute pas le professeur.

   — _____

2. —Marc n'apprend pas les nouveaux mots.

   — _____

3. —Marc ne fait pas ses devoirs.

   — _____

➤➤➤➤➤➤

4. —Marc ne lit pas le livre de littérature.

   — _____

5. —Marc ne recopie pas ses notes.

   — _____

6. —Marc ne finit jamais son travail.

   — _____

7. —Marc ne comprend pas les problèmes de maths.

   — _____

8. —Marc n'utilise pas son ordinateur.

   — _____

E. Qu'est-ce qu'on va faire? The Goberts are on vacation. The children mention things they are interested in and the parents are willing to do them. Write the parents' responses using **aller** + direct object pronouns and the infinitive in parentheses.

Modèle —J'aime ce livre. (acheter)
        ➤ —On va l'acheter, alors.

1. —On dit que ce film est excellent. (voir)

   — _____

2. —Il y a un bon restaurant français dans ce quartier. (chercher)

   — _____

3. —J'ai envie de voir les musées. (visiter)

   — _____

4. —Le poisson est très bon ici. (essayer)

   — _____

5. —Les cartes postales sont prêtes _(ready)_. (envoyer)

   — _____

6. —Le train n'est pas encore là. (attendre)

   — _____

7. —Voilà la serveuse du restaurant de notre hôtel. (saluer)

—_____

8. —Avec cette voiture-là on peut visiter la ville. (louer)

—_____

F. **La classe de français.** Complete the following paragraph with the missing direct object pronouns to describe what is happening in French class today.

Dans la classe de français les étudiants ne tutoient pas le professeur. Ils

_____ (1) vouvoient. Mais, lui, il _____ (2) tutoie. Luc voit ses copains quand

il arrive et il _____ (3) salue en français. Le professeur commence à parler.

—Nous ne _____ (4) entendons pas, monsieur, disent les étudiants. Vous parlez

trop doucement (_softly_). —Bon, je répète, répond le professeur. Mais vous

devez _____ (5) écouter avec attention. —Tu _____ (6) comprends? demande

Luc à Claire. —Oui, un peu. Il emploie les nouveaux mots du vocabulaire et

je ne _____ (7) sais pas. —Monsieur, dit Luc, —pouvons-nous réviser le

vocabulaire avant de continuer? —Bon, si vous voulez. Il y a beaucoup de

nouveaux mots et vous allez _____ (8) répéter après moi.

IV. The Use and Formation of the Imperative

■ The imperative or command form of the verb can be used to tell someone to do something or not to do something. The imperative is formed by dropping the subject pronoun **tu, nous,** or **vous** from the present tense. The imperative of the **nous** form means _let's do something._

Statement	Imperative
Tu finis tes devoirs. _You're finishing your homework._	**Finis** tes devoirs. _Finish your homework._
Tu ne pars pas maintenant. _You're not leaving now._	**Ne pars pas** maintenant. _Don't leave now._
Nous rentrons. _We are going home._	**Rentrons.** _Let's go back._
Nous n'attendons plus. _We're not waiting any longer._	**N'attendons plus.** _Let's not wait any longer._
Vous restez chez vous. _You're staying at home._	**Restez** chez vous. _Stay home._
Vous ne descendez pas. _You're not going downstairs._	**Ne descendez pas.** _Don't go downstairs._

■ In the imperative of the **tu** form of **-er** verbs, the **-s** of the ending is dropped. This includes the irregular verb **aller** and **-ir** verbs conjugated like **-er** verbs such as **ouvrir** and **offrir**.

Statement	Imperative
Tu joues avec ton petit frère.	**Joue** avec ton petit frère.
You play with your little brother.	*Play with your little brother.*
Tu vas à l'école.	**Va** à l'école.
You go to school.	*Go to school.*
Tu n'ouvres pas la porte.	**N'ouvre pas** la porte.
You don't open the door.	*Don't open the door.*

■ The verbs **avoir** and **être** have irregular command forms.

	AVOIR	ÊTRE
tu	aie	sois
nous	ayons	soyons
vous	ayez	soyez

G. Les bons conseils de maman. Little Georges is starting first grade. What advice does his mother give him? Use the **tu** form of the imperative of the phrases given to repeat what she tells him.

Modèle ne pas arriver en retard
➤ N'arrive pas en retard.

Pour donner de bons conseils

l'album (de bandes dessinées) *comic book*

les conseils *(masc. pl.) advice*

être sage *to be good (said of children)*

faire des fautes *to make mistakes*

jeter quelque chose par terre *to throw something on the floor/ground*

lisiblement *legibly*

mâcher du chewing-gum *to chew gum*

noter *to jot down, write down*

---

1. être sage

_____

2. ranger tes affaires sur ton pupitre

_____

3. ne pas parler avec les autres élèves

_____

4. ne rien manger dans la salle de classe

_____

5. ne rien jeter par terre

_____

6. écouter attentivement le professeur

_____

7. écrire lisiblement

_____

8. ne pas apporter tes albums à l'école

_____

H. Les conseils du professeur. Georges's older sister Joséphine is in her first year at a **collège** (French junior high or middle school). The history teacher gives his class advice on the first day. To repeat what he tells his students, use the **vous** form of the imperative of the phrases given.

Modèle   ne pas arriver en retard
➤ N'arrivez pas en retard.

1. noter soigneusement vos devoirs

_____

2. essayer de comprendre les idées

_____

3. lire attentivement

_____

4. ne pas mâcher de chewing-gum en classe

_____

5. apporter vos livres et un cahier

_____

6. ne pas perdre votre temps

_____

➤➤➤➤➤

7. ne jamais bavarder pendant la leçon

_____

8. ne pas avoir peur de me poser *(ask)* des questions

_____

I. Des projets pour samedi soir. A group of friends is making plans for Saturday evening. To repeat the suggestions of the different members of the group, write the **nous** form of the imperative of the phrases given.

Modèle   sortir en groupe samedi soir
   ➤ Sortons en groupe samedi soir.

1. aller au cinéma

_____

2. ne pas voir de film

_____

3. prendre des billets *(tickets)* pour le concert

_____

4. rendre visite à Madeleine

_____

5. ne pas passer la soirée chez elle

_____

6. faire de la barque au lac du parc

_____

7. aller voir les animaux au zoo

_____

8. manger au café du zoo. Quelle bonne idée!

_____

J. **Il faut aller faire des choses.** Use the imperative of the verb of motion in parentheses to tell a friend or friends what they should go to do.

Modèles —Je dois travailler? (aller)
➤ —Oui, va travailler.

—Nous devons travailler? (venir)
➤ —Oui, venez travailler.

1. —Je dois manger? (venir)

— _____

2. —Nous devons acheter à manger? (descendre)

— _____

3. —Je dois chercher le dictionnaire? (monter)

— _____

4. —Nous devons faire nos devoirs? (rentrer)

— _____

5. —Je dois faire du jogging? (sortir)

— _____

6. —Nous devons lire le journal? (aller)

— _____

7. —Je dois préparer le déjeuner? (revenir)

— _____

8. —Nous devons rendre visite à Hélène? (passer)

— _____

K. Des conseils aux copains. Serge has advice for his friends and himself. Change these sentences with **il faut** *(it is necessary to)* or **il ne faut pas** *(one, we shouldn't, mustn't)* to the **nous** form of the imperative to repeat what he tells them.

Modèles   Il faut travailler.
➤ Travaillons.

Il ne faut pas attendre.
➤ N'attendons pas.

1. Il faut être travailleurs.

_____

2. Il ne faut pas oublier qu'il y a un examen demain.

_____

3. Il ne faut pas avoir peur de l'examen.

_____

4. Il faut commencer à étudier.

_____

5. Il faut essayer de réviser toutes les notes.

_____

6. Il ne faut pas perdre notre temps.

_____

7. Il faut étudier ensemble.

_____

8. Il faut apprendre beaucoup de choses par cœur.

_____

V. Object Pronouns with the Imperative

■ In the affirmative imperative (telling someone to do something), object pronouns follow the imperative form and are attached to it with a hyphen.

—Je dois acheter ce livre?	*Should I buy this book?*
—Oui. **Achète-le.**	*Yes. **Buy it.***
—Nous pouvons attendre les copains?	*May we wait for our friends?*
—Oui, bien sûr. **Attendez-les.**	*Yes, of course. **Wait for them.***

■ The pronoun **me** becomes **moi** when it follows a command form.

—**Aidez-moi.** Je ne comprends rien.	***Help me.** I don't understand anything.*
—**Attendez-moi** là-bas. J'arrive tout de suite.	***Wait for me** there. I'll get there right away.*

■ The final **-s** of the **tu** form that is lost in the imperative of **-er** verbs is restored (and pronounced) before the pronouns **y** and **en:**

—Oh, des bonbons. J'adore ça!	*Oh, candy. I love it (candy).*
—Manges-**en.**	*Eat some.*
—Je suis très bien dans cette pièce.	*I'm so comfortable in this room.*
—Restes-**y.**	*Stay there.*

■ In the negative imperative (telling someone not to do something), object pronouns appear in their normal position before the conjugated verb or before the infinitive in a verb + *infinitive* construction.

—J'ai de nouveaux albums. Regarde-les.	*I have some new comics. Look at them.*
—**Ne me dérangez pas.** J'ai trop de travail.	***Don't bother me.** I have too much work.*

L. Vas-y! *(Go ahead!)* Use the informal imperative and an object pronoun, **y** or **en** to offer your friend the things he is interested in.

Modèle   —J'aime bien ta nouvelle cassette. Je peux l'écouter?
    ➤ —Oui, écoute-la!

1. —Tu as des chocolats. Je peux les manger?

   — _____

2. —Ah, une nouvelle revue française. Je peux la regarder?

   — _____

3. —Une lettre de notre ami Jean-Claude! Je peux l'ouvrir?

   — _____

➢➢➢➢➢

4. —Tout le monde a soif. Je dois remplir les verres?

— _____

5. —Je voix des fautes dans ta composition. Je dois les corriger?

— _____

6. —Tu as un nouveau album de Tintin! Je peux le lire?

— _____

7. —Tu veux ces sandwichs? Je dois les emballer *(wrap)*?

— _____

8. —Je dois parler avec Solange. Je peux la voir?

— _____

M. Non, pas ça. Tell your friends not to do what they ask in each case using the negative imperative (**vous** form) and an object pronoun corresponding to the words in italics. Then suggest an alternative using the affirmative imperative and an object pronoun.

Modèle   —Nous devons rendre *ce livre* à la bibliothèque? (prêter à Philippe)
➤ —Ne le rendez pas à la bibliothèque. Prêtez-le à Philippe.

Quelques nouveaux verbes

garder *to keep*

déposer *to drop off, to let off*

laisser *to let, to leave*

laisser quelqu'un tranquille
to leave someone alone

rentrer le chat *to bring in the cat*

1. —Nous devons parler *à Mireille* maintenant? (appeler ce soir)

— _____

2. —Nous devons recopier *nos notes*? (lire encore une fois)

— _____

3. —Nous pouvons laisser *le chat* dehors. (rentrer)

— _____

4. —Nous devons ranger *ces vêtements.* (laisser sur le lit)

— _____

5. —Nous devons servir *cette eau minérale*? (boire)

   —_____

6. —Nous devons *te* déposer en ville? (raccompagner)

   —_____

7. —Nous devons garder *cette vieille bicyclette*? (vendre)

   —_____

8. —Nous pouvons *t'*aider? (laisser tranquille)

   —_____

N. Va le faire. Tell your friend what to do by using the verbs in parentheses and the appropriate object pronoun corresponding to the words in italics. Your answers to your friend will have a familiar imperative in the verb + *infinitive* construction.

Modèle —Je ne trouve pas *mon manteau*. (aller/chercher dans le placard [*closet*])
➤ —Va le chercher dans le placard.

1. —Je n'ai pas mes lunettes. (rentrer/chercher)

   —_____

2. —Nous avons beaucoup de *mots* à étudier. (commencer à/apprendre maintenant)

   —_____

3. —J'ai envie de parler à *Grégoire*. (aller/rendre visite)

   —_____

4. —*Sylvie* est seule dans la cuisine. (monter/aider à faire la cuisine)

   —_____

5. —J'ai envie de bavarder avec *ton frère et toi*. (venir/voir cet après-midi)

   —_____

6. —Il y a beaucoup de *fautes* dans ma composition. (essayer de/corriger)

   —_____

➤➤➤➤➤

7. —*Jacques* m'attend dans la rue. (descendre/voir)

   — _____

8. —Il va pleuvoir et *les fenêtres* de mon appartement sont ouvertes!
   (rentrer/fermer)

   — _____

O. Décisions. Two friends are deciding what to do. In each case the suggestion is in the **nous** form of the imperative, either affirmative or negative as indicated. Write out the decisions about what to do using the appropriate object pronouns.

Modèles   —On prend un peu de cette tarte aux pommes? (oui, manger)
➤ —Oui, mangeons-en.

—On prend un peu de cette tarte aux pommes? (non, manger)
➤ —Non, n'en mangeons pas.

1. —On prend *les billets* pour le concert, n'est-ce pas? (oui, prendre)

   — _____

2. —On a besoin des *livres de Claude,* n'est-ce pas? (non, emprunter)

   — _____

3. —On va voir *le musée,* n'est-ce pas? (oui, visiter)

   — _____

4. —On va voir notre professeur de géographie? (non, déranger)

   — _____

5. —On a beaucoup de mots à apprendre, n'est-ce pas? (oui, étudier)

   — _____

6. —On doit demander à Jean s'il veut venir? (non, inviter)

   — _____

7. —On a encore besoin de ces vieux papiers? (oui, garder)

   — _____

8. —On doit acheter *les journaux,* n'est-ce pas? (oui, acheter)

   — _____

P. Composition. Make a list in French of six things you would like to do with a friend or friends. Then propose four things to a friend that you and that person can do together.

Passé composé with *avoir*; Object Pronouns in the passé composé

I. Formation and Use of the Passé composé

■ The French **passé composé** covers the meanings of the English simple past *(I spoke)* and the English present perfect *(I have spoken)*. Like the English present perfect, the French **passé composé** is composed of an auxiliary verb (**avoir** [*have*]) and past participle (**parlé** [*spoken*]).

■ French past participles are formed as follows.

-**Er** verbs change the -**er** of the infinitive to -**é**:
parler ➤ **parlé**, trouver ➤ **trouvé**

-**Ir** verbs change the -**ir** of the infinitive to -**i**:
finir ➤ **fini**, choisir ➤ **choisi**

-**Re** verbs change the -**re** of the infinitive to -**u**:
répondre ➤ **répondu**, vendre ➤ **vendu**

■ Study the conjugation of **parler** in the **passé composé**.

PARLER *TO SPEAK*

singular	plural
j'ai parlé	nous avons parlé
tu as parlé	vous avez parlé
il/elle/on a parlé	ils/elles ont parlé

■ Some verbs have irregular past participles.

apprendre ➤ **appris**	découvrir ➤ **découvert**	ouvrir ➤ **ouvert**
avoir ➤ **eu**	devoir ➤ **dû**	pouvoir ➤ **pu**
boire ➤ **bu**	dire ➤ **dit**	prendre ➤ **pris**
comprendre ➤ **compris**	écrire ➤ **écrit**	savoir ➤ **su**
connaître ➤ **connu**	être ➤ **été**	voir ➤ **vu**
courir ➤ **couru**	faire ➤ **fait**	vouloir ➤ **voulu**
couvrir ➤ **couvert**	lire ➤ **lu**	
croire ➤ **cru**	mettre ➤ **mis**	

A. On prend rendez-vous. Lise and Claudine arranged to meet at their favorite café yesterday. Find out how they made their arrangements by rewriting each of the following sentences in the **passé composé**.

Modèle Lise travaille à la maison.
    ➤ Lise a travaillé à la maison.

1. Lise finit ses devoirs.

_____

2. Elle téléphone à son amie Claudine.

_____

3. Le téléphone sonne et Claudine répond.

_____

4. Les deux amies bavardent un peu.

_____

5. Elles décident d'aller au centre-ville.

_____

6. Claudine propose un rendez-vous au «Café des Sportifs».

_____

7. Elles raccrochent et mettent leurs manteaux.

_____

8. Lise prend l'autobus et Claudine prend le métro.

_____

B. La journée de Marc Duval. What did Marc Duval do yesterday? Construct sentences in the **passé composé** out of the words given to tell about his day.

Modèle Marc/faire beaucoup de choses hier
    ➤ Marc a fait beaucoup de choses hier.

1. Marc/passer la journée à l'école

_____

2. il/retrouver ses amis à la sortie de l'école

_____

3. ils/parler de leurs cours

_____

4. Marc et ses amis/jouer au football

_____

5. ensuite, ils/prendre quelque chose au café

_____

6. tout le monde/décider de rentrer

_____

7. ils/faire leurs devoirs

_____

8. Marc/regarder la télé avant d'aller au lit

_____

C. **Quelle bonne classe!** Mme Mercier has a very good class. The students have already done everything that was supposed to be done. Write the students' answers to the teacher's questions in the **passé composé.** Use the word **déjà** in the answers. (**Déjà** is placed between the auxiliary verb **avoir** and the past participle.)

Modèle —Vous allez étudier le vocabulaire, n'est-ce pas?
➤ —Nous avons déjà étudié le vocabulaire, madame.

1. —Jean-Claude, vous allez écrire une composition, n'est-ce pas?

— _____

2. —Aimée et Justine, vous allez lire le chapitre seize, n'est-ce pas?

— _____

3. —Et Luc, il va apporter ses disques de chansons françaises, n'est-ce pas?

— _____

4. —Et Solange, elle va rédiger une lettre en français, n'est-ce pas?

— _____

➤➤➤➤➤➤

5. —Stéphane, vous allez apprendre le vocabulaire par cœur, n'est-ce pas?

    —_____

6. —Françoise, vous allez répondre à toutes les questions, n'est-ce pas?

    —_____

7. —Charles, vous allez ouvrir les fenêtres, n'est-ce pas?

    —_____

8. —Vivienne et Véra, vous allez ranger les livres sur l'étagère, n'est-ce pas?

    —_____

D. Un samedi plein d'activité. Look at the following pictures and tell what Suzanne and her friends Sophie and Nicole did last Saturday. Select from the following expressions and write your sentences in the **passé composé.**

Les activités

écouter de nouveaux disques compacts

essayer des vêtements dans un magasin

faire une randonnée

jouer au basket-ball

parler du film

prendre quelque chose au café

retrouver des amis au centre

voir un film

---

1. _____   2. _____

   _____   _____

3. _____

   _____

4. _____

   _____

5. _____

   _____

6. _____

   _____

7. _____

   _____

8. _____

   _____

II. Negatives and Questions in the Passé composé

■ The negative of the **passé composé** is formed by placing **ne** before the conjugated form of **avoir** and **pas** (or **rien, jamais, plus**) after the form of **avoir** and before the participle.

—Tu **n'as pas** compris le message de Hans?	*Didn't you understand Hans's message?*
—Non, je **n'ai rien** compris. Je **n'ai jamais** fait d'allemand, tu sais.	*No, I didn't understand **anything**. I **never** studied German, you know.*

■ The negative word **personne** *follows* the past participle.

—Vous **n'avez pas** vu Marie?	*You didn't see Marie?*
—Non, nous **n'avons** vu **personne.**	*No, we **didn't** see **anyone**.*

■ To form questions with inversion in the **passé composé,** invert the subject pronoun and the auxiliary verb.

—**As-tu parlé** avec Marie?	*Did you speak with Marie?*
—Non. **A t-elle téléphoné?**	*No. Did she call?*

■ In everyday speech, question words may come at the end of the sentence.

Tu as fini **quand**?	*When did you finish?*
Il a acheté **combien de** chocolat?	*How much chocolate did he buy?*
Elles ont nagé **où**?	*Where did they swim?*

E. **Quelle classe paresseuse!** M. Guibert is not as lucky as Mme Mercier. The students in his class haven't done anything yet. Write his questions and his students' answers using the **passé composé.** The students' answers will be in the negative with the word **encore** between the negative word **pas** and the past participle.

Modèles Suzanne/vous /écouter les cassettes ➤
—Suzanne, est-ce que vous avez écouté les cassettes?
—Non, Monsieur. Je n'ai pas encore écouté les cassettes.

Serge/lire l'article ➤
—Est-ce que Serge a lu l'article?
—Non, Monsieur. Il n'a pas encore lu l'article.

1. Maurice et Paul/vous/préparer les conversations

   — _____

   — _____

2. Jacques/ouvrir le laboratoire de langues

   — _____

   — _____

3. Alain/vous/étudier la grammaire

— _____

— _____

4. Guy et Frédéric/rendre les livres à la bibliothèque

— _____

— _____

5. Chantal/finir les devoirs

— _____

— _____

6. Michèle et Élisabeth/choisir un livre

— _____

— _____

7. Claire/vous/acheter le journal français

— _____

— _____

8. Marc et Christine/vous/trouver vos cahiers

— _____

— _____

F. **Une journée ratée** (*A day gone wrong*). No one was able to do what he or she planned today. Tell what people did not do using the negative of the **passé composé.**

Modèle   Christine/téléphoner à ses amies
➢ Christine n'a pas téléphoné à ses amies.

1. moi/faire du jogging

_____

2. Jacques/retrouver ses amis en ville

_____

➢➢➢➢➢

3. Odile et Michèle/choisir un cadeau pour Elvire

_____

4. toi et moi/jouer au volley-ball

_____

5. Monique/visiter le musée d'art

_____

6. Paulette et toi/rendre visite à vos grands-parents

_____

7. toi/écrire une lettre à Françoise

_____

8. moi/passer la journée à la campagne

_____

G. Absolument rien. These people haven't done anything today. Say so using **ne... rien** and the **passé composé.**

Modèle   Philippe/faire
          ➢ Philippe n'a rien fait.

1. toi/lire

_____

2. Charles et Richard/écrire

_____

3. Barbara/acheter

_____

4. nous/vendre

_____

5. vous/entendre

_____

6. Émilie et Véronique/trouver

_____

7. ta mère/envoyer

_____

8. moi/voir

_____

H. Personne. Nobody was where they were expected to be. Say that these people found, saw, and met nobody. Use **ne... personne** and the **passé composé.** Remember that the negative word **personne** follows the past participle.

Modèle Christian/voir
    ➤ Christian n'a vu personne.

1. mes copains/retrouver

_____

2. moi/rencontrer

_____

3. Françoise/entendre

_____

4. toi/déranger

_____

5. le professeur/ennuyer

_____

6. nous/aider

_____

7. vous/oublier

_____

8. Paul et Lise/saluer

_____

III. Object Pronouns in the Passé composé

■ Object pronouns *precede* the auxiliary verb **avoir** in the **passé composé**:

—**Marc** n'est pas absent?   *Marc isn't absent?*
—Non, je **l'**ai vu à la cantine.   *No, I saw **him** in the lunchroom.*

—Vous connaissez **cette chanson?**   *Do you know **this song?***
—Oui, nous **l'**avons entendue.   *Yes, we have heard **it.***

—Elle aime **ses nouveaux gants?**   *Does she like **her new gloves?***
—Oui, elle **les** a mis aujourd'hui.   *Yes, she put **them** on today.*

■ The negative word **ne** precedes the object pronoun.

—Tu as **le paquet?**   *Do you have the **package?***
—Non, je **ne l'**ai pas reçu.   *No, I **didn't** receive **it.***

—On ne **t'**a pas appelé?   *They (people) **didn't** call **you?***
—Non, on **ne m'**a pas contacté.   *No, they **didn't** contact **me.***

■ When a direct object pronoun is used with the **passé composé**, the past participle agrees with the direct object pronoun in gender and number. These endings are silent unless the participle ends in a consonant, which will be pronounced in the feminine singular and feminine plural.

—Tu as vu **Marie?**   *Did you see **Marie?***
—Non, je ne **l'**ai pas vue.   *No, I didn't see **her.***

—Vous avez vu **les fermes?**   *Did you see **the farms?***
—Oui, on **les** a visitées.   *Yes, we visited **them.***

—**Lise, Paulette,** vous n'allez pas à la boum?   ***Lise, Paulette,** aren't you going to the party?*
—On ne **nous** a pas invitées.   *They didn't invite **us.***

—Josette ne porte pas **sa nouvelle robe.**   *Josette is not wearing **her new dress.***
—Pourquoi est-ce qu'elle ne **l'**a pas mise?   *Why didn't she put **it** on?*

—Tu as fini **ta leçon?**   *Did you finish **your lesson?***
—Oui, je **l'**ai faite.   *Yes, I did **it.***

Note:

The indirect object pronouns such as **lui, leur** and the pronouns **y** and **en** do not cause agreement of the past participle: Rachelle? Je **lui** ai **écrit.**

I. **La boum va être formidable!** Isabelle is organizing this Saturday night's party. She is checking with Gérard to make sure people have done what they were supposed to. In each case, Gérard tells her that each person has accomplished his or her task. Write Gérard's answers using the **passé composé** and the object pronoun corresponding to the words in italics. Make the past participle agree with any direct object pronouns.

Modèle   —Philippe a acheté *les gobelets?*
  ➤ Oui, il les a achetés.

1. —As-tu contacté *Christelle et Monique?*

   —_____

2. —Rachelle a-t-elle préparé *les hors-d'œuvres?*

   —_____

3. —Louis et Jacques ont-ils nettoyé *le salon?*

   —_____

4. —Marcelle a-t-elle mis *la table?*

   —_____

5. —Yvette et toi, est-ce que vous avez coupé *le fromage* en cubes?

   —_____

6. —Est-ce que ta mère a fait *les boulettes de viande?*

   —_____

7. —Est-ce que Jocelyne a servi *le jus de pommes?*

   —_____

8. —Est-ce que tu as invité *Sylvie?*

   —_____

J. Jamais! Deny that these things ever happened. Use **ne… jamais,** the **passé composé,** and an object pronoun corresponding to the words in italics. Make the past participle agree with any direct object pronouns.

Modèle   —Tu as souvent écouté *cette cassette,* n'est-ce pas?
➤ —Non, je ne l'ai jamais écoutée.

1. —Marc a dérangé *les autres étudiants,* n'est-ce pas?

    — _____

2. —Moi, je *t'*ai souvent aidé, n'est-ce pas?

    — _____

3. —Brigitte a lu *cette histoire* aux enfants, n'est-ce pas?

    — _____

4. —Paul et Cécile ont vu *leur vieille tante,* n'est-ce pas?

    — _____

5. —Tu as souvent pris *le métro,* n'est-ce pas?

    — _____

6. —André a souvent conduit *la voiture de son père,* n'est-ce pas?

    — _____

7. —Ta grand-mère a promené *le chien,* n'est-ce pas?

    — _____

8. —Tu as prêté *ta mobylette* à Claude, n'est-ce pas?

    — _____

K. Une année en Afrique. Complete this story about Sandrine's new job in Senegal by adding the verbs in the **passé composé.** Make all necessary agreements. Her story begins with a letter.

La mère de Sandrine _____ (1. laisser) la lettre sur la table de

la salle à manger. Sandrine l'_____ (2. trouver) et elle l'_____

(3. ouvrir). Elle l'_____ (4. lire). Le gouvernement du Sénégal lui

_____ (5. offrir) un travail de professeur dans une école de Dakar.

Elle va enseigner le français et la géographie. Sandrine _____

(6. commencer) tout de suite à faire ses valises. Le directeur de l'école où

elle va enseigner l'_____ (7. appeler). Sandrine et le directeur

_____ (8. parler) de l'école et des élèves. Sandrine _____

(9. décider) de partir pour le Sénégal au mois d'août pour avoir le temps

de chercher un appartement. Elle _____ (10. acheter) un billet d'avion

pour Dakar. Elle va sûrement passer une année très intéressante en Afrique.

L. Questions personnelles. Answer the following questions in the **passé composé.**

1. Qu'est-ce que vous avez fait ce week-end?

   _____

2. Qu'est-ce que vous avez acheté?

   _____

3. À quels jeux vos amis et vous avez-vous joué?

   _____

4. Combien d'heures avez-vous étudié?

   _____

5. À qui avez-vous téléphoné?

   _____

6. Est-ce que vous avez entendu de nouvelles chansons? Quelles chansons?

   _____

M. Composition. Write a composition of six or seven sentences about what you and your friends did yesterday, or last week, or on the weekend. Use the **passé composé** (trying to avoid verbs of motion, **aller, venir,** etc. since they are *not* conjugated with **avoir,** as you will see in Chapter 16). Use words like **après, ensuite,** and phrases such as **quand on a fini** to link your sentences.

Definite and Partitive Articles; Boire; Quantity Words

I. Partitive Article

■ Before singular nouns such as **argent** *(money)*, **lait** *(milk)*, or **eau** *(water)* that cannot take an indefinite article, French uses a partitive article to indicate an indefinite quantity. Study the forms of the partitive article.

Masculine	Feminine	Nouns beginning with a vowel or a mute *h*
du lait *milk*	**de la** viande *meat*	**de l'**argent *money*
du café *coffee*	**de la** salade *salad*	**de l'**eau *water*

—Tu veux **du** lait?   *Do you want (**some**) milk?*
—Non, je veux **de l'**eau.   *No, I want (**some**) water.*

■ In the plural, the partitive has the same form as the plural of the indefinite article: **des œufs** *(eggs)*, **des frites** *(french fries)*.

■ After a negative the partitive article, like the indefinite article, becomes **de** (**d'** before a vowel or a mute **h**).

—Tu **ne** prends **pas de** lait?   *You're **not** having **any** milk?*
—Non, je **ne** veux **pas de** lait.   *No, I **don't** want **any** milk.*
—**De l'**eau, peut-être?   ***Some** water, perhaps?*
—Non, je **ne** veux **pas d'**eau, merci.   *No, I **don't** want **any** water, thanks.*

■ When a noun can be preceded by both the partitive article and the indefinite article, the meaning is different.

de la viande *some meat*	**une** viande *a type of meat*
du fromage *some cheese*	**un** fromage *a whole cheese*
du café *some coffee*	**un** café *a cup of coffee*

■ The partitive is often used with verbs such as **manger, prendre** *(to have something to eat or drink)*, **demander** *(to ask for)*, etc.

—Le matin je **mange du pain.**   *In the morning I **eat bread.***
—Avec **du beurre**?   *With **butter**?*
—Non, avec **de la confiture.** Et toi?   *No, with **jam.** What about you?*
—Je **ne mange pas de pain.** Je   *I **don't eat (any) bread.** I **have***
   prends **du lait,** c'est tout.   *(some) milk, that's all.*

■ Other verbs, such as **aimer** and **préférer,** are usually followed by a definite article showing that the noun is used in a general sense.

—Tu **aimes le poulet**?   *Do you **like chicken**?*
—Oui, mais je **préfère le poisson.**   *Yes, but I **prefer fish.***

A. **Le petit déjeuner.** Serge and some friends are having breakfast at the school cafeteria today. He tells what each one is having. Create sentences out of each string of words.

Modèle   Jacques/prendre/café
> Jacques prend du café.

Le petit déjeuner

les céréales *(fem. pl.) cereal*	le lait *milk*
la confiture *jam*	le miel *honey*
le chocolat *hot chocolate*	l'œuf *(masc.) egg*
le jambon *ham*	le sucre *sugar*
le jus d'orange *orange juice*	le thé *tea*

---

1. Monique et Suzanne/manger/céréales/avec/lait

   _____

2. Colette/manger/pain/avec/confiture

   _____

3. Michel/prendre/jus d'orange

   _____

4. Jocelyne et Vivienne/manger/œufs/avec/jambon

   _____

5. Guillaume/prendre/thé/avec/sucre

   _____

6. Alfred et Christine/manger/fruits

   _____

7. moi/manger/pain/avec/beurre/et/miel

   _____

8. notre professeur/prendre/café

   _____

B. Au restaurant. Complete these conversations between servers and their customers by adding the missing partitive or definite articles.

> ### Au restaurant
>
> l'agneau *(masc.) lamb*
>
> le bœuf *beef*
>
> le coq au vin *chicken braised in red wine*
>
> le fromage *cheese*
>
> le gazeux *sparkling water, mineral water*
>
> les* hors-d'œuvre *(masc. pl)* *hors d'oeuvres, first course*
>
> le pâté *pâté, goose liver pâté*
>
> le poisson *fish*
>
> le poulet *chicken*
>
> le repas *meal*
>
> le saucisson *sausage, salami*
>
> le serveur *waiter*
>
> la serveuse *waitress*
>
> le veau *veal*
>
> la viande *meat*
>
> le vin *wine*
>
> ———
>
> *Indicates aspirate **h**, that is, there is no elision (**le hamburger**).

a. SERVEUSE: Qu'est-ce que vous désirez comme hors-d'œuvre, madame?

    _____ (1) saucisson?

    CLIENTE: Non, pas _____ (2) saucisson aujourd'hui. Je voudrais

    _____ (3) pâté.

b. SERVEUR: _____ (4) viande, monsieur?

    CLIENT: Non, pas _____ (5) viande. Je préfère _____ (6) poisson.

    Vous avez _____ (7) poisson?

c. CLIENT: Je veux manger _____ (8) viande ce soir.

    SERVEUSE: Bien. _____ (9) agneau ou _____ (10) bœuf?

d. SERVEUR: Vous voulez prendre _____ (11) vin avec votre repas,

    mademoiselle?

    CLIENTE: Merci, mais je ne prends pas _____ (12) vin. _____ (13)

    gazeux, s'il vous plaît.

e. SERVEUR: Si vous voulez prendre _____ (14) poulet, le coq au vin est

    excellent.

    CLIENTE: C'est une bonne idée, mais je préfère _____ (15) veau.

f. SERVEUSE: Et comme dessert? _____ (16) fromage?

    CLIENT: Non, je ne veux pas _____ (17) fromage. Vous pouvez

    m'apporter _____ (18) fruits?

Au café et au restaurant

- If you order a **citron pressé** (lemonade) at a café, the waiter will squeeze the lemons in front of you into a glass. You add water and sugar to taste.
- In French houses, coffee is served in the morning in a bowl, usually black coffee. This is called **un bol de café.**
- Although **une tarte** is often translated as *pie,* it is quite different from an American pie. A tarte is usually an individual pastry, open on top, made with slices of fruit. Note that the preposition **à** is used to label the main ingredient: **une tarte aux pommes, une tarte aux poires, une tarte aux fraises,** etc.

C. Au régime. Jean-Luc is trying to lose weight. He refuses all the desserts his mother offers him. Note that **merci** often means *no, thank you* in French.

Modèle (gâteau) ➤
—Tu veux du gâteau?
—Merci, maman, pas de gâteau pour moi.

1. glace

   — _____

   — _____

2. chocolat

   — _____

   — _____

3. bonbons

   — _____

   — _____

4. tarte aux pommes

   — _____

   — _____

5. tarte aux poires

   — _____

   — _____

➤➤➤➤➤

6. crème caramel

   — _____

   — _____

7. fraises à la crème

   — _____

   — _____

8. mousse au chocolat

   — _____

   — _____

II. *Boire*

■ The verb **boire** *(to drink)* is commonly followed by a noun with the partitive article. **Boire** is irregular.

BOIRE *TO DRINK*

singular		**plural**	
je	bois	nous	buvons
tu	bois	vous	buvez
il/elle/on	boit	ils/elles	boivent

D. Quelle soif! *(How thirsty they are!)* This group of friends has been working in the garden on a hot summer day. What do they have to drink after they finish?

Modèle   Philippe/eau
   ➤ Philippe boit de l'eau.

1. Véronique/thé glacé

   _____

2. Papa/bière

   _____

3. moi/limonade

   _____

4. toi/café glacé

_____

5. Annette et Lise/orange pressée

_____

6. vous/jus de pommes

_____

7. nous/jus d'orange

_____

8. mes petits frères/lait

_____

III. Quantity Words

- Most words that tell how much or how many are connected to the following noun by **de** (**d'**) without the article.

assez de (**d'**) *enough*

autant de (**d'**) *as much, as many*

beaucoup de (**d'**) *much, many, a lot of*

Combien de (**d'**)? *How much? How many?*

peu de (**d'**) *little, few, not much, not many*

tant de (**d'**) *so much, so many*

trop de (**d'**) *too much, too many*

un peu de (**d'**) *a little*

- Quantity expressions are also formed with nouns. These are also connected to the following noun by **de** (**d'**) without the article.

une boîte de *a box of*

une bouteille de *a bottle of*

un kilo de *a kilogram (2.2 pounds) of*

un litre de *a liter of*

une livre de *a pound of (usually ½ kilogram)*

une tasse de *a cup of*

un verre de *a glass of*

—**Combien de** lait voulez-vous, madame?

—**Une bouteille de** lait et **un litre de** vin.

*How **much** milk do you want, madam?*

*A **bottle of** milk and **a liter of** wine.*

E. Liste de courses. *(Shopping list)*. Alice is going to do the shopping for her mother. Here is her list in note form. Write out each item as a phrase.

Modèle lait: 1 bouteille
     ➢ une bouteille de lait

1. veau : 1 kilo
2. beurre : 1 livre
3. salade : un peu
4. fruits : beaucoup
5. jus de pommes : 1 litre
6. thé : 1 petite boîte
7. saucisson : 1 kilo
8. bonbons : 1 boîte

1. _____

2. _____

3. _____

4. _____

5. _____

6. _____

7. _____

8. _____

F. Pour préciser. Add the quantity expressions in parentheses to each sentence and make all necessary changes to the form of the partitive article.

Modèle Je veux du lait. (un verre)
     ➢ Je veux un verre de lait.

1. Tu dois acheter des chocolats pour les enfants. (beaucoup)

    _____

2. Nous allons préparer du veau pour tout le monde. (assez)

    _____

3. Je vais boire du thé. (une tasse)

    _____

4. La mère a du lait pour ses enfants. (un litre)

    _____

5. On va acheter des poires. (une livre)

    _____

6. Tu veux de l'eau? (un verre)

    _____

7. Grand-père veut boire du vin. (un peu)

    _____

8. En général, je mange de la viande. (peu)

    _____

G. **Composition.** Write about what you eat and drink during the day, where and with whom. Use the verbs **manger, prendre,** and **boire,** and the following vocabulary.

Des aliments

pour le petit déjeuner *for breakfast*	**les haricots verts** *(masc. pl.) green beans*
pour le déjeuner *for lunch*	**le légume** *vegetable*
pour le dîner *for dinner*	**les pâtes** *(fem. pl.) pasta*
pour le goûter *for afternoon (after-school) snack*	**les petits pois** *(masc. pl.) peas*
la carotte *carrot*	**la pizza** *pizza*
les frites *(fem. pl.) french fries*	**la pomme de terre** *potato*
le hamburger *hamburger*	**la salade** *lettuce, salad*

Indirect Object Pronouns; Υ and en

I. Indirect Object Nouns

■ Indirect object nouns in French refer to people. They answer the question *to whom* and are connected to the verb by the preposition **à.**

Les étudiants **répondent au professeur.**	*The students **answer the teacher.***
J'écris **à mes cousins.**	*I write (to) my cousins.*

In the above sentences, **au professeur** and **à mes cousins** are the indirect objects of the verbs **répondent** and **écris.**

■ Many verbs can be followed by both a direct object noun and an indirect object noun. In these cases the direct object noun is a thing and the indirect object noun is a person.

Je donne **la lettre à François.**	*I give **François the letter.*** *(or: I give **the letter to François.**)*
Monique offre **un foulard à sa mère.**	*Monique gives **her mother a scarf** (as a gift).*

The direct objects in the above sentences are **la lettre** and **un foulard.** The indirect objects are **à François** and **à sa mère.**

II. Indirect Object Pronouns

■ Indirect object pronouns in French replace objects consisting of the preposition **à** plus an animate noun, that is, a noun referring to a person. Study the indirect object pronouns in French.

	singular	plural
first person	me, m'	nous
second person	te, t'	vous
third person	lui	leur

Notes:

1. The indirect object pronouns for the first and second persons are the same as the direct object pronouns. **Me** and **te** become **m'** and **t'** before a vowel or mute **h.**

2. The pronoun **lui** means both *to him* and *to her.*

—Qu'est-ce que tu vas offrir à Solange pour son anniversaire?	*What are you going to give Solange for her birthday?*
—Je vais **lui** offrir un foulard.	*I'm going to give **her** a scarf.*

—Je vois que Paul a une voiture.	*I see that Paul has a car.*
—Oui, sa mère **lui** prête sa voiture.	*Yes. His mother lends **him** her car.*
—Tu lis souvent à tes petits cousins?	*Do you often read to your little cousins?*
—Oui, je **leur** lis des livres pour enfants.	*Yes, I read children's books **to them**.*

■ Study the following verbs and expressions commonly occurring with indirect objects. In these constructions **quelqu'un** stands for any animate noun (a noun referring to a person) and **quelque chose** stands for any inanimate noun (a noun referring to a thing).

a. Verbs that take indirect objects in French but not in English

> **aller (bien) à quelqu'un** *to look nice on someone (said of articles of clothing)*
>
> **obéir à quelqu'un** *to obey someone*
>
> **répondre à quelqu'un** *to answer someone*
>
> **téléphoner à quelqu'un** *to call, phone someone*

—Tu crois que ce chapeau **me** va?	*Do you think this hat looks nice **on me**?*
—Ah, oui, il **te** va très bien.	*Oh yes, it looks great **on you**.*
—Voici une lettre de Janine. Tu vas **lui** répondre?	*Here's a letter from Janine. Are you going to answer **her**?*
—Oui. Je **lui** téléphone tout de suite.	*Yes. I'll telephone **her** right away.*

b. Some verbs take an inanimate direct object and an animate indirect object in French.

> **apporter quelque chose à quelqu'un** *to bring something to someone*
>
> **dire quelque chose à quelqu'un** *to say/tell something to someone*
>
> **écrire (quelque chose) à quelqu'un** *to write (something) to someone*
>
> **expliquer quelque chose à quelqu'un** *to explain something to someone*
>
> **montrer quelque chose à quelqu'un** *to show something to someone*
>
> **rendre quelque chose à quelqu'un** *to return something to someone*

■ Note that **demander quelque chose à quelqu'un** *(to ask someone for something)* works like the expressions above. The inanimate noun (the thing asked for) is the direct object and the animate noun (the person asked) is the indirect object.

Pierre demande **une voiture à ses parents.**	*Pierre asks **his parents for a car**.*

A. Des amies généreuses. Louise and Paulette are always willing to help their friends out. Write what they say they will do in each case using **on,** the verb and noun in parentheses, and the appropriate indirect object pronoun.

Modèle   Samuel n'a pas de crayon. (donner/un de nos crayons)
➢ On lui donne un de nos crayons, alors.

1. Jean-Luc et Georges n'ont pas de voiture. (prêter/notre voiture)

   _____

2. Christine veut acheter un livre de chimie. (vendre/ton vieux livre de chimie)

   _____

3. C'est l'anniversaire de Carole. (offrir/un chemisier)

   _____

4. Sandrine et Marthe ont besoin de mille francs. (rendre/leurs mille francs)

   _____

5. Mme Duval ne peut pas descendre faire les courses. (apporter/du pain et du fromage)

   _____

6. Nicolas ne comprend pas la leçon de maths. (expliquer/les problèmes)

   _____

7. Bernard cherche la maison de Sylvie. (dire/son adresse)

   _____

8. Les Bertin veulent déménager. (trouver/un appartement)

   _____

B. Jamais. None of the things asked about ever happens. Answer these questions in the negative using **ne... jamais** and the appropriate indirect object pronoun. Repeat any direct object nouns in your answer.

Modèle   —Est-ce que tes cousins obéissent *à leurs parents?*
➢ —Non, ils ne leur obéissent jamais.

1. —Est-ce que Maurice *t'*écrit?

   — _____

2. —Est-ce que Vivienne *te* dit la vérité?

   — _____

3. —Est-ce que Mlle Sarda parle *à Jean-Claude* en français?

   — _____

4. —Est-ce que Luc téléphone *à Nadine?*

   — _____

5. —Est-ce que tu réponds *à François* quand il te parle?

   — _____

6. —Est-ce que tu prêtes de l'argent *à tes copains?*

   — _____

7. —Est-ce que nous demandons leurs notes *à nos camarades de classe?*

   — _____

8. —Est-ce que ton chien *t'*apporte le journal?

   — _____

C. **Qu'est-ce qu'on va faire?** Write what people are going to do in each of the following situations. Use **devoir** + infinitive, the words in parentheses, and an indirect object pronoun.

Modèle   —Zoé veut parler avec toi. (je/téléphoner)
        ➤ —Je dois lui téléphoner.

1. —Hervé veut voir tes photos. (je/montrer mon album)

   — _____

2. —Solange n'a pas de vélo. (Claude/vendre sa bicyclette)

   — _____

3. —Tes grands-parents veulent savoir si tu vas bien. (je/écrire)

   — _____

4. —Jacques est malade et ne va pas au lycée. (nous/apporter nos notes)

   — _____

5. —Je ne comprends pas ces problèmes de chimie. (je/expliquer comment les faire)

   — _____

➤➤➤➤➤➤

6. —Suzanne et Janine veulent téléphoner à Lucille. (nous/donner son numéro de téléphone)

   — _____

7. —C'est l'anniversaire de mon cousin à Paris. (tu/envoyer un cadeau)

   — _____

8. —Marc a de nouveaux jeux vidéo. (on/demander ses jeux)

   — _____

D. Questions personnelles. Answer each of the following questions in French, making sure to have a direct or an indirect object pronoun in each answer.

1. Qu'est-ce qu'on va vous offrir pour votre anniversaire?

   _____

2. Qu'est-ce que vous allez offrir à votre père/mère/frère/sœur/meilleur(e) ami(e) pour son anniversaire?

   _____

3. Qu'est-ce que vous dites à vos amis quand vous les voyez le matin?

   _____

4. À qui demandez-vous de l'argent quand vous voulez acheter quelque chose?

   _____

5. Dans quelle langue répondez-vous au professeur s'il vous pose une question en français?

   _____

6. Téléphonez-vous souvent à vos amis?

   _____

7. Est-ce que vous invitez souvent vos amis chez vous?

   _____

8. Est-ce que vous lisez souvent le journal?

   _____

II. The Pronoun *y*

- The indirect object pronouns in French replace phrases consisting of the preposition **à** + an animate noun (a noun referring to a person).

  Je réponds **au professeur**. ➤   Je **lui** réponds.

  Le professeur répond **aux étudiants**. ➤ Il **leur** répond.

- However, if there is a phrase consisting of the preposition **à** + an inanimate noun (a noun referring to a thing), it is replaced not by an indirect object pronoun but by the pronoun **y. Y** can replace both singular and plural nouns. **Y,** like the direct and indirect object pronouns, is placed before the conjugated verb, but before the infinitive in the verb + infinitive construction.

  Le professeur répond **aux questions**. ➤ Le professeur **y** répond.

- Phrases with **à** most often tell *where*.

—Est-ce que Mireille est **à la gare**?	*Is Mireille **at the train station**?*
—Oui, elle **y** attend son train.	*Yes, she's waiting for her train (**there**). (**y** = à la gare)*
—Elle va **à Paris**?	*Is she going **to Paris**?*
—Oui, elle **y** va deux fois par semaine.	*Yes, she goes **there** twice a week. (**y** = à Paris)*
—Tu vas **à Paris** aussi?	*Are you going **to Paris** too?*
—Non, je ne peux pas **y** aller.	*No, I can't go (**there**). (**y** = à Paris)*

- **Y** can also replace phrases beginning with other prepositions of location such as **dans, sur, sous, chez.**

—Le chat est **sur le lit**?	*Is the cat **on the bed**?*
—Oui, il **y** dort.	*Yes, he's sleeping (**there**).*
—Qu'est-ce que tu trouves **dans le tiroir**?	*What do you find **in the drawer**?*
—J'**y** trouve des papiers.	*I find (sheets of) paper (**there, in it**).*

E. Quand ça? Answer the following questions about when people are doing certain things using the cues in parentheses and replacing the phrases in italics by either **y** or the appropriate indirect object pronoun.

Modèle   —Quand est-ce que Jean va *en Suisse*? (la semaine prochaine)
     ➤ —Il y va la semaine prochaine.

1. —Quand est-ce que Michèle téléphone *à ses amis*? (tous les jours)

   — _____

2. —Quand est-ce que tu veux aller *à la piscine*? (demain)

   — _____

3. —Quand est-ce que Robert et Stéphane retournent *à l'école*? (après-demain)

   — _____

➤➤➤➤➤

4. —Quand est-ce que Barbara peut parler *au professeur?* (vendredi)

—_____

5. —Quand est-ce que Louis écrit *à ses amis?* (pendant les vacances)

—_____

6. —Quand est-ce que vous allez *au cinéma,* Richard et toi? (dimanche)

—_____

7. —Quand est-ce que le car arrive *à la gare routière?* (dans une heure)

—_____

8. —Quand est-ce que tu rentres *au bureau?* (à deux heures)

—_____

F. **Qu'est-ce qu'on y fait?** Use the verb in parentheses to tell what these people are doing at different places around town. Replace the phrases in italics appropriately in your answers.

Modèle —Qu'est-ce que vous faites *à la piscine?* (nager)
➤ —Nous y nageons.

1. —Qu'est-ce que vous faites *au café?* (prendre un thé)

—_____

2. —Qu'est-ce que tu cherches *dans le placard?* (mon manteau)

—_____

3. —Qu'est-ce que le chat fait *sous la table?* (dormir)

—_____

4. —Qu'est-ce que les étudiants font *à la bibliothèque?* (faire leurs devoirs)

—_____

5. —Qu'est-ce que tu fais *au laboratoire de langues?* (écouter des cassettes)

—_____

6. —Qu'est-ce que vous faites *à la cantine?* (manger)

—_____

7. —Qu'est-ce que Marie et Jeanne font *dans le bureau*? (travailler)

   —_____

8. —Qu'est-ce que vous faites *sur le terrain de sport*? (jouer au football)

   —_____

G. **Mon chien.** Julie tells what her dog does during the day. Complete each of her statements by looking at the pictures and selecting one of the verbs or phrases from the list that precedes the exercise. Replace the phrases in italics appropriately.

La vie d'un chien

aboyer *to bark*

la balle *ball (smaller than a soccer ball)*

courir *to run* (**je cours, tu cours, il court, nous courons, vous courez, ils courent**)

la flaque d'eau *puddle*

le gazon *lawn*

image *reflection*

rester *to stay, remain*

le trottoir *sidewalk*

Modèle

Mon chien est *dans la cuisine*. (manger)
➢ Il y mange.

1. Mon chien entre *dans la salle de séjour*.

   _____

2. Il est *sur le canapé*.

_____

3. Il sort *au jardin*.

_____

4. Il est *dans la piscine*.

_____

5. Il y a un gazon *devant la maison*.

_____

6. Il y a une flaque d'eau *sur le trottoir*.

_____

7. Il va *dans la cuisine*.

_____

8. Mon chien va *sous la table*.

_____

IV. The Pronoun *en*

■ The pronoun **en** can replace most phrases beginning with **de** (**du, de la, de l', des**). It can replace the partitive.

—Je vais boire **du lait.** Tu **en** veux?   *I'm going to drink **some milk.** Do you want **any**?*

—Merci, mais je n'**en** bois presque jamais.   *No thanks. I almost never drink **any**.*

—Tu veux **du jus d'orange**?   *Do you want **any orange juice**?*

—Si tu **en** as, j'**en** prends.   *If you have (**any**), I'll have **some**.*

En may or may not be translated into English, but it is necessary in the French sentences.

■ **En** replaces phrases beginning with **de** after quantity words.

—Vous avez **du fromage**?	*Do you have **any cheese**?*
—Oui, j'**en** ai beaucoup.	*Yes, I have **a lot** (**of it**).*
	(**en** = beaucoup de fromage)
—Combien est-ce que vous **en** avez?	*How much (**of it**) do you have?*
	(**en** = combien de fromage?)
—J'**en** ai **un kilo**.	*I have **a kilogram** (**of it**).*
	(**en** = un kilo de fromage)

■ **En** also replaces nouns (animate or inanimate) that follow numbers even though no **de** is present:

—Tu as **un chat**?	*Do you have **a cat**?*
—J'**en** ai **deux**.	*I have **two** (**of them**).*
	(**en** = deux **chats**)
—Combien d'étudiants y a-t-il dans cette classe?	*How many students are there in this class?*
—Il y **en** a **vingt-huit**.	*There are **twenty-eight**.*
	(**en** = 28 étudiants)

■ **En** also replaces phrases with **de** when the preposition means *about* or *from* or is part of an idiom such as **avoir besoin de**.

—Il va parler **de son voyage**?	*Is he going to speak **about his trip**?*
—Oui, il aime **en** parler.	*Yes, he likes to talk **about it**.*
	(**en** = du voyage)
—Quand revient-elle **de Belgique**?	*When is she coming back **from Belgium**?*
—Elle **en** revient demain.	*She is coming back (**from there**) tomorrow.* (**en** = de Belgique)
—Tu veux **ton stylo**?	*Do you want **your pen**?*
—Oui, j'**en** ai besoin.	*Yes, I **need it**.* (**en** = de mon stylo)

H. Histoires d'aliments. Rewrite the answers in each of the following exchanges replacing the word or phrase in italics appropriately.

Modèle   —Tu veux du pain?
   —Merci, je ne veux pas *de pain*.
   ➤ Merci, je n'en veux pas.

1. —Si tu vas au marché, tu peux prendre des bananes.
   —Je vais acheter quatre *kilos de bananes*.

   — _____

2. —Pardon, Mme Deschênes. Vous avez des pommes? Nous, on n'en a pas.
   —Oui, Mme Masson, mais je n'ai pas beaucoup *de pommes*. Vous pouvez prendre trois *pommes*.

   — _____

3. —Je descends au marché. Tu veux du jus d'ananas?
   —Oui, je veux une bouteille *de jus d'ananas.*

   — _____

4. —Maman va faire du riz avec le poulet?
   —Oui, elle va faire *du riz.*

   — _____

5. —Est-ce que nous avons besoin de légumes?
   —Oui, nous avons besoin *de légumes.* Nous n'avons plus *de légumes.*

   — _____

6. —Pourquoi est-ce que tu ne finis pas ton lait, Jean-Pierre?
   —Je n'ai pas envie *de lait,* maman.

   — _____

7. —Mais tu sais que je déteste les petits pois, maman.
   —Mais tu dois manger *des petits pois,* Nathalie.

   — _____

8. —On mange beaucoup de maïs chez toi aux États-Unis?
   —Oui, on mange beaucoup *de maïs.*

   — _____

I. **Non, merci.** Turn down all these kind offers using the negative of the verb in parentheses and the pronoun **en.** Notice the use of **merci** to mean *no thank you.*

Modèle   —Tu veux du vin? (boire/jamais)
           ➤ —Merci, mais je n'en bois jamais.

1. —Je te prête de l'argent? (avoir besoin/pas)

   — _____

2. —Ton petit frère veut des haricots verts? (manger/pas)

   — _____

3. —Tu veux une de mes revues allemandes? (lire/plus)

   — _____

4. —Je te prépare du café? (avoir envie/pas)

   — _____

➤➤➤➤➤

5. —J'ai beaucoup de cassettes de rock. Tu en veux? (écouter/plus)

   — _____

6. —J'achète des écharpes en laine pour toi? (porter/plus)

   — _____

7. —Je achète des feutres pour ta sœur? (employer/jamais)

   — _____

8. —On aide Marie avec sa composition? (écrire/pas)

   — _____

J. **Marie-Claire et son père.** Complete the following story about Marie-Claire's visit to her father at work with the pronouns **y** and **en.**

Modèle   Marie-Claire va voir son père à deux heures et demie aujourd'hui. Son bureau est au centre-ville. Marie-Claire prend le métro pour __y__ arriver.

Au centre-ville	
la confiserie *candy store, sweetshop*	**penser** *to think*
content de *happy with*	**la vitrine** *shop window*

1. Marie-Claire mange dans un café du centre-ville. Elle ____ reste une heure.

2. Le café fait de bons sandwichs. Marie-Claire ____ mange un.

3. À deux heures elle quitte le café pour le bureau de son père. Elle ____ va à pied.

4. Elle passe devant une confiserie. La vitrine est très belle. Marie-Claire ____ voit des bonbons merveilleux.

5. Elle veut ____ acheter pour son père.

6. La confiserie est ouverte. Elle ____ entre.

7. Elle ____ sort avec une boîte de chocolats belges.

8. Elle pense que son père va être très content du cadeau. Et elle a raison.

   Il ____ est très content.

K. À la campagne. Olivier is visiting his friend Grégoire who lives on a farm near Poitiers. Complete Grégoire's answers to Olivier's questions with the pronouns **y** and **en**.

Note: French uses different words for *to grow* when talking about what the farmer does (e.g., *The farmer grows wheat*) and what the plant does (e.g., *Wheat grows in this region*). For the farmer's activity, use **cultiver** or **faire pousser** in French. For the plants, use **pousser**.

Dans notre ferme nous **cultivons le blé.**	*On our farm we **grow wheat.***
Ma mère **fait pousser des tomates.**	*My mother **grows tomatoes.***
Le riz ne pousse pas dans notre région.	*Rice **doesn't grow** in our region.*

1. —Cultivez-vous du blé?

   —Oui, on ____ cultive dans ce champ-là.

2. —Et le maïs? Vous faites pousser du maïs aussi?

   —Non, on n'____ cultive pas.

3. —Il y a une écurie?

   —Oui, nous ____ gardons nos chevaux.

4. —Vous avez un vignoble?

   —Non, nous n'____ avons pas. Nous ne cultivons pas le raisin.

5. —J'aime bien les tomates, tu sais.

   —Tu as de la chance. Maman ____ fait pousser dans le jardin potager.

6. —Qu'est-ce qu'il y a dans cet enclos?

   —Rien, pour le moment, mais demain tu vas ____ voir nos chèvres.

7. —Vous avez beaucoup de chèvres?

   —Nous ____ avons quarante-cinq.

8. —Mais toi, tu n'es plus à la ferme. Tu es à l'université, à Poitiers,

   n'est-ce pas?

   —Oui. J'____ fais de l'agronomie!

L. Olivier écrit à sa famille. Complete Olivier's letter to his parents about his stay on Grégoire's family's farm by adding the missing object pronouns: direct, indirect, **y,** or **en.**

Mes chers parents,

   Comment allez-vous? Je _____ (1) salue de Poitou. Je suis chez Grégoire maintenant, et sa ferme est très jolie. Je _____ (2) aime bien. La vie à la campagne est très intéressante. Grégoire est très patient. Je _____ (3) pose beaucoup de questions et il _____ (4) répond. Il _____ (5) explique beaucoup de choses sur la vie à la campagne. Sa ferme est grande. On _____ (6) cultive du blé mais pas de maïs. On _____ (7) élève beaucoup d'animaux aussi. Il y a des chèvres et surtout beaucoup de moutons. Ils _____ (8) ont plus de deux cents, je crois!

   Les légumes ici sont toujours frais parce que sa mère _____ (9) fait pousser dans son jardin potager. Vous n'allez pas me croire, mais j'_____ (10) mange beaucoup, même des petits pois! Dans quelques semaines les fruits du verger seront (will be) mûrs. Grégoire _____ (11) dit que les pêches et les prunes sont vraiment délicieuses! Je vais _____ (12) rapporter à Paris.

   Et j'ai une surprise pour vous. L'année prochaine je ne vais pas à la faculté de médecine. Je veux faire de l'agronomie et acheter une ferme en Poitou. Que pensez-vous de mon idée?

Je vous embrasse,

Olivier

M. Des questions pour vous. Answer these personal questions using an object pronoun in your answers.

1. Combien de livres apportez-vous à l'école tous les jours?

   _____

2. Allez-vous souvent à la bibliothèque?

   _____

3. Téléphonez-vous souvent à vos amis?

   _____

4. Où achetez-vous vos vêtements?

   _____

5. Combien d'étudiants y a-t-il dans votre classe de français?

   _____

6. Passez-vous beaucoup de temps à la cantine?

   _____

7. Vos amis viennent-ils souvent vous voir?

   _____

8. Aimez-vous les légumes?

   _____

N. Composition. Imagine you live on a farm. Describe a typical day for you helping out with the chores. If you do live on a farm, tell what you do in fact do. Write five or six sentences and try to use object pronouns wherever you can.

Passé composé with être;
Word Order in the passé composé

I. The Passé composé with *être*

■ Many verbs of motion in French form the **passé composé** with **être**, not **avoir**, as the helping or auxiliary verb. When a verb is conjugated with **être**, the past participle agrees in gender and number with the subject of the sentence. Study the conjugation of **arriver** in the **passé composé**. Note that the chart gives the various possibilities of agreement. For instance, **je suis arrivé(e)** means that a man writes **je suis arrivé** and a woman writes **je suis arrivée**. The pronunciation is the same.

ARRIVER *TO ARRIVE*

singular	plural
je **suis** arrivé(e)	nous **sommes** arrivé(e)s
tu **es** arrivé(e)	vous **êtes** arrivé(e)(s)
il **est** arrivé	ils **sont** arrivés
elle **est** arrivée	elles **sont** arrivées

■ When a verb is conjugated with **être**, the past participle is masculine singular with the pronoun **on** when **on** means *people, one* but agrees in gender and number (masculine plural or feminine plural) when **on** means *we*.

On **est arrivé** en retard.　　　　*People arrived late.*
On **est arrivé(e)s** en retard.　　　*We arrived late.*

■ The following common verbs are conjugated with **être** in the **passé composé**.

aller ➢ je suis allé(e)　　　　　　rentrer ➢ je suis rentré(e)

arriver ➢ je suis arrivé(e)　　　　rester ➢ je suis resté(e)

descendre ➢ je suis descendu(e)　retourner ➢ je suis retourné(e)

devenir ➢ je suis devenu(e)　　　revenir ➢ je suis revenu(e)

entrer ➢ je suis entré(e)　　　　sortir ➢ je suis sorti(e)

monter ➢ je suis monté(e)　　　venir ➢ je suis venu(e)

partir ➢ je suis parti(e)

A. Le déménagement. The whole family helped the Marchands move yesterday. Tell what each person did using the **passé composé** with **être.**

Modèle   Maurice Marchand/aller louer le camion
       ➢ Maurice Marchand est allé louer le camion.

Le déménagement

la boîte en carton *cardboard box*	**faire la malle** *to pack the trunk*
le camion *truck*	**la penderie** *walk-in closet*
le grenier *attic*	**le sous-sol** *basement*
la malle *trunk (piece of luggage)*	

---

1. Corinne/descendre au sous-sol

   _____

2. les grands-parents/rester dans la cuisine

   _____

3. la tante Aurélie/monter au grenier

   _____

4. l'oncle Julien/venir faire les malles

   _____

5. Maurice/revenir avec le camion

   _____

6. Charlotte et Jeanne/entrer dans les penderies

   _____

7. Mme Marchand/aller chercher des boîtes en carton

   _____

8. le chien et le chat/sortir jouer dans le jardin

   _____

B. L'élève souffrant. Guillaume was home from school yesterday with a twisted ankle. Tell what his day was like using the **passé composé,** distinguishing between verbs using **avoir** and verbs using **être** as the helping verb.

Guillaume _____ (1. ne pas aller) au collège hier.

Il _____ (2. rester) chez lui. Il _____ (3. passer)

la journée dans sa chambre. Il _____ (4. ne pas descendre).

Sa mère lui _____ (5. apporter) ses repas. Après le collège, ses

amis _____ (6. venir) le voir. Guillaume _____

(7. être) content de les voir. Ils lui _____ (8. acheter) un

nouveau album de bandes dessinées. Ils lui _____ (9. donner)

une liste de ses devoirs aussi. Ses professeurs lui _____

(10. écrire) des notes. Guillaume les _____ (11. lire) avec

beaucoup de plaisir. Ses amis _____ (12. partir) à cinq heures,

et Guillaume _____ (13. commencer) à faire ses devoirs. À six

heures et demie, son père _____ (14. monter) avec son dîner.

C. Conversations au passé. Create exchanges out of the strings of words given. Form questions in the **passé composé** using **est-ce que** and a response that incorporates the answer in parentheses. Replace words in italics by the appropriate object pronoun in the answer.

Modèle   quand/Jean/aller/*au marché* (hier) ➤
             —Quand est-ce que Jean est allé au marché?
             —Il y est allé hier.

1. pourquoi/ta sœur/monter/*à sa chambre* (parce que/est fatiguée)

   — _____

   — _____

2. quand/le directeur/arriver/*à l'école* (il y a cinq minutes)

   — _____

   — _____

3. où/tu/prendre/*l'autobus* (devant le lycée)

   — _____

   — _____

4. quand/tes copines/rentrer/*de la campagne* (avant-hier)

   — _____

   — _____

5. où/vous (Marc et toi)/acheter/*ces cartes de Noël* (au centre commercial)

   — _____

   — _____

6. combien/*lait*/tu/boire (beaucoup)

   — _____

   — _____

7. quand/l'avion/partir/*de Genève* (à huit heures du soir)

   — _____

   — _____

8. qui/venir/*te* voir (Henri et Hervé)

   — _____

   — _____

II. Word Order in the Passé composé

■ Object pronouns precede the helping verb.

Tu **m'**as téléphoné.	*You called **me**.*
Nous **y** sommes restés.	*We stayed **there**.*

■ **Ne** precedes the helping verb (or the object pronoun if there is one) and **pas** and other negative words follow the helping verb.

Tu **ne** m'as **pas** téléphoné.	*You **didn't** call me.*
Nous **n'**y sommes **plus** restés.	*We **didn't** stay there **anymore**.*

■ The negative word **personne** follows the past participle.

Je n'ai vu **personne**.	*I didn't see **anybody**.*

■ The rules for the position of adverbs in the **passé composé** are complex. Adverbs of place follow the past participle in both French and English.

—Est-ce que vous avez étudié **ici**?   *Did you study **here**?*
—Non, nous avons étudié **en haut**.   *No, we studied **upstairs**.*

- Many adverbs of time such as **aujourd'hui, hier, avant, après,** etc. follow the past participle or come at the beginning of the sentence.

  Je suis parti **après.** ⎫
  Après je suis parti. ⎭   *I left **afterwards**.*

- The adverbs **bien, mal, déjà, toujours** precede the past participle, as do adverbs of quantity.

  —Ils sont **déjà** revenus?   *Have they come back **yet**?*
  —Oui, ils ont **beaucoup** voyagé.   *Yes, they traveled **a great deal**.*

  —Je vois que tu n'as pas **assez** dormi.   *I see that you didn't sleep **enough**.*
  —Oui, j'ai **trop** mangé hier et j'ai   *Yes, I ate **too much** yesterday and*
     mal dormi.   *I slept **badly**.*

- The adverbs **bientôt, encore, longtemps, rarement, récemment, souvent, tout de suite** usually precede the past participle.

  —Vous avez **souvent** visité ce musée?   *Did you **often** visit that museum?*
  —Non, j'y suis **rarement** allé.   *No, I **seldom** went there.*

- Many adverbs in -**ment** can either precede or follow the past participle.

  Il a écouté **attentivement.** ⎫
  Il a **attentivement** écouté. ⎭   *He listened **attentively**.*

D. Expansion. Rewrite the following sentences adding the adverbs in parentheses.

1. Merci, tu m'as aidé. (beaucoup)

   _____

2. Excusez-moi, j'ai compris. (mal)

   _____

3. Il a couru. (ici)

   _____

4. Nous avons parlé. (longtemps)

   _____

5. Je t'ai écrit. (souvent)

   _____

6. Il m'a déposé à la gare. (toujours)

   _____

7. Nous avons fermé les fenêtres. (tout de suite)

   _____

8. Les enfants ont joué. (dehors)

   _____

E. **Quels problèmes pour arriver à son travail!** Rewrite this story about Marie's rushed morning in the **passé composé,** paying special attention to agreements with the past participle and to the position of adverbs and negative words.

1. Marie sort vite de chez elle.

   _____

2. Elle va tout de suite à l'arrêt de l'autobus.

   _____

3. L'autobus ne vient pas encore.

   _____

4. Elle ne prend jamais un taxi pour aller au bureau.

   _____

5. Elle attend longtemps l'autobus.

   _____

6. Elle voit des taxis partout.

   _____

7. Aujourd'hui elle appelle un taxi.

   _____

8. Elle n'arrive pas tard au bureau.

   _____

F. **Composition.** Write about you and your family or you and your friends. Tell where you all went last weekend, using as many verbs of motion as possible. Tell when you went to the different places and what you did there. Write six or seven sentences.

Faire; Expressions with faire and avoir

I. Faire

■ Study the conjugation of the verb **faire** *(to make, to do)*.

singular	plural
je fais	nous faisons
tu fais	vous faites
il/elle/on fait	ils/elles font

■ Some common expressions with **faire**

faire attention *to pay attention*

faire la cuisine *to cook, to do the cooking*

faire la vaisselle *to do the dishes*

faire le jardin *to do the gardening*

faire le linge *to do the laundry*

faire le lit (**faire les lits**) *to make the bed (to make the beds)*

faire le ménage *to do the housework*

faire les courses *to do the marketing, run the day's errands*

faire ses devoirs *to do one's homework*

A. Une recette simple (A simple formula). These students know how to do well at school. They pay attention in class and do their homework in the evening. Use the expressions **faire attention** and **faire ses devoirs** to talk about their recipe for success. Don't use stressed pronouns in this exercise.

Modèle Antoinette ➤
Antoinette fait attention en classe. Le soir, elle fait ses devoirs.

1. Paul et Michel _____

2. je _____

3. ces filles _____

4. nous _____

5. Olivier _____

6. vous _____

7. tu _____

B. Beaucoup de travail chez les Duval. Sophie Duval comes from a large family. She talks about what each member of her family does to help out. Write what she says using the indicated expression with **faire.** Use stressed pronouns followed by the subject pronoun where indicated.

Modèle maman/beaucoup de travail
> Maman fait beaucoup de travail.

1. moi/le linge

   _____

2. mon petit frère/son lit

   _____

3. ma sœur Mireille/la vaisselle

   _____

4. mon frère, ma sœur et moi/le jardin

   _____

5. mes grands-parents/le ménage

   _____

6. maman/la cuisine

   _____

II. *Faire* with the Partitive

■ **Faire** is used with the partitive article and school subjects to mean *to study.*

faire de la chimie *to study chemistry*

faire du français *to study French*

faire de l'informatique *to study computer science*

La spécialisation

The construction **faire** + *partitive article* + *subject* can also be used as the equivalent of *to major in a subject* when talking about the university. Since French students get their general education at the **lycée,** they usually study only their area of specialization at the university. Thus, a computer science major studies computer science and related subjects exclusively and would describe his or her work at the university as **Je fais de l'informatique.**

■ **Faire** is used with the partitive article and the names of activities, especially sports, that are individual efforts. (For team sports, French uses **jouer à.**)

faire du sport *to play sports, participate in sports*

faire du vélo, de la bicyclette *to bike ride*

faire du piano, du violon *to take piano, violin lessons*

—Marguerite **fait de l'exercice,**   *Marguerite **exercises**, doesn't she?*
    n'est-ce pas?
—Ah, oui, elle **fait du jogging** et   *Yes, she **jogs** and **bikes.***
    du vélo.

■ Quantity words can be added to these expressions.

—Je suis très fatigué.   *I'm very tired.*
—C'est que tu fais **trop d'**exercice.   *That's because you exercise **too much.***
—Je fais **un peu de** vélo, c'est tout.   *I do a **little** bike riding, that's all.*
—Un peu? Hier tu as fait **vingt**   *A little? Yesterday you rode **twenty***
    kilomètres.   *kilometers.*

C. Les loisirs. Tell what these students do in their free time by creating sentences with the correct form of the verb **faire.** Use quantity words and stressed pronouns where indicated.

Modèle   mes frères/camping ➤ Mes frères font du camping.

1. Lucien/vélo

        _____

2. Marcelle/beaucoup/patin à roulettes

        _____

3. moi/natation

        _____

4. Chantal et Odile/six kilomètres à pied tous les jours

        _____

5. toi/un peu/voile

        _____

6. Bernard et moi/photographie

        _____

7. vous/randonnées à la montagne

        _____

D. Quelle activité? Find an expression in column B for each definition in column A.

A

_____ 1. faire du sport dans l'eau

_____ 2. faire dix kilomètres à pied

_____ 3. employer un appareil-photo

_____ 4. prendre des leçons de musique

_____ 5. ranger les vêtements pour un voyage

_____ 6. faire du vélo

B

a. faire les valises

b. faire de la bicyclette

c. faire du violon

d. faire une randonnée

e. faire de la natation

f. faire de la photographie

III. Weather Expressions with *faire*

■ French uses the verb **faire** to talk about the weather. Most weather expressions begin with the impersonal phrase **il fait**.

Note:

An impersonal expression has no real subject. In other words, you can't tell who is performing the action. A dummy subject (*it* in English, **il** in French) is used to fill the gap in the sentence. Compare English *It's sunny* and French **Il fait du soleil.**

Quel temps fait-il? *What's the weather like?*

Il fait beau. *The weather's nice.*

Il fait froid. *It's cold.*

Il fait frais. *It's cool.*

Il fait du soleil. *It's sunny.*

Il fait du vent. *It's windy.*

Il fait du brouillard. *It's foggy.*

Il fait mauvais. *The weather's bad.*

Il fait chaud. *It's hot, warm.*

Il fait gris. *It's overcast.*

Quelle température fait-il? *What's the temperature?*

Il fait 65 degrés. *It's 65 degrees (Fahrenheit).*

■ To express *very* with weather expressions use **très** before **beau, mauvais, chaud, froid, frais, gris,** and **beaucoup de** (not **du**) before the nouns **soleil, vent,** and **brouillard.**

■ Some weather expressions without **faire**

Il pleut. *It's raining.*

Il pleut beaucoup. *It rains a lot.*

Il va pleuvoir. *It's going to rain.*

Il neige. *It's snowing.*

Il neige beaucoup. *It snows a lot.*

Il va neiger. *It's going to snow.*

E. Les activités et le temps. Using the adverb **quand** *(when)* and a weather expression, describe what these people do in different types of weather.

Hervé

Modèle   Quand il neige, Hervé fait du violon.

Louise

Jean-Luc

1. _____

2. _____

_____

Isabelle et Robert

Chantal

3. _____

4. _____

_____

_____

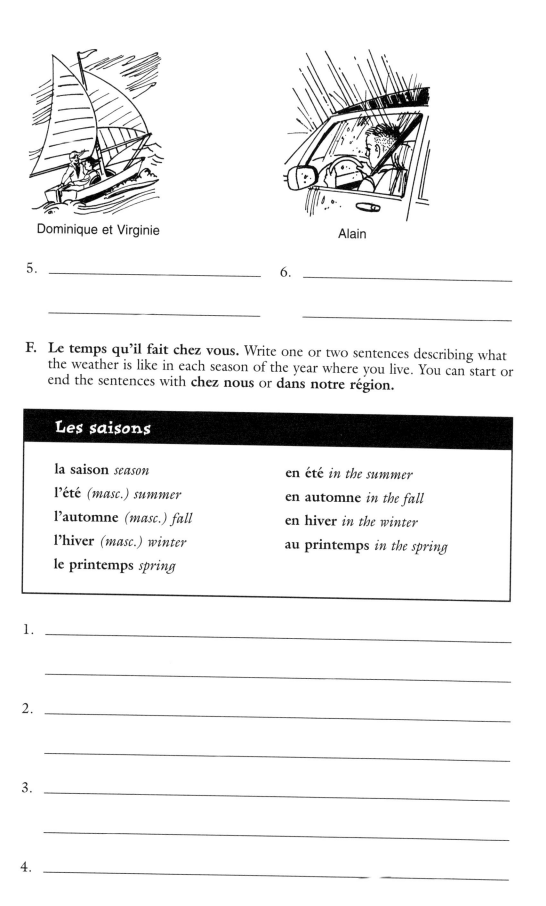

Dominique et Virginie

Alain

5. _____ 6. _____

_____ _____

F. Le temps qu'il fait chez vous. Write one or two sentences describing what the weather is like in each season of the year where you live. You can start or end the sentences with **chez nous** or **dans notre région.**

Les saisons

la saison *season*	en été *in the summer*
l'été *(masc.) summer*	en automne *in the fall*
l'automne *(masc.) fall*	en hiver *in the winter*
l'hiver *(masc.) winter*	au printemps *in the spring*
le printemps *spring*	

1. _____

_____

2. _____

_____

3. _____

_____

4. _____

_____

G. **Votre activité et le temps.** Think of five activities expressed with **faire** that you like or don't like to do depending on the weather. Write about your preferences using phrases such as **j'aime faire, je n'aime pas faire, je déteste faire, je préfère faire, j'adore faire,** etc.

Modèles   Je n'aime pas faire mes devoirs quand il fait beau.

          or

          Je préfère faire mes devoirs quand il fait gris.

1. _____

2. _____

3. _____

4. _____

5. _____

IV. Expressions with *avoir*

■ Many French expressions consisting of **avoir** + *a noun* are the equivalents of English expressions consisting of *to be* + *an adjective.*

avoir faim *to be hungry*	**avoir froid** *to be cold*
avoir soif *to be thirsty*	**avoir raison** *to be right*
avoir sommeil *to be sleepy*	**avoir tort** *to be wrong*
avoir chaud *to be warm*	**avoir de la chance** *to be lucky*

■ Some expressions with **avoir** take **de** before a following noun.

avoir besoin de *to need*	**avoir honte (de)** *to be ashamed (of)*
avoir envie de *to feel like*	

—Est-ce que tu **as faim?**	*Are you **hungry?***
—Oui, j'**ai envie de** prendre une glace.	*Yes, I **feel like** having an ice cream.*
—Marc ne va pas bien?	*Marc isn't feeling well?*
—Non, il **a froid** et il **a sommeil.**	*No, he's **cold** and **sleepy.***
—J'ai **besoin d'**un stylo.	*I **need** a pen.*
—Tu **as de la chance.** Moi, j'ai deux stylos aujourd'hui.	*You're **lucky.** I have two pens today.*

■ **Avoir** is also used to express age.

—**Quel âge avez-vous?**	*How old are you?*
—J'**ai seize ans.**	*I'm sixteen years old.*

■ Other expressions use **être** + *adjective.*

être fâché(e) (contre) *to be angry* **être malade** *to be sick*
  (with)
être fatigué(e) *to be tired* **être pressé(e)** *to be in a hurry*

être fou *(fem.* **folle,** *masc. pl.* **fous)**
  to be crazy

H. **Après l'excursion.** Cléo's class has just returned from a long school trip. Express how the students feel in French. Use stressed pronouns where necessary.

1. Sophie is sleepy.

   _____

2. *I'm* hungry.

   _____

3. Léo and I are thirsty.

   _____

4. *You're* cold. *(informal)*

   _____

5. Philippe feels like going back home.

   _____

6. You and Monique are lucky. You have candy.

   _____

7. You're right, Cléo. We're not hungry.

   _____

8. The teacher needs to have a cup of coffee.

   _____

I. **Tant de verbes!** Complete the following paragraph with the correct forms of **avoir, être, aller, faire,** or **prendre.**

Luc et Sophie _____ (1) manger au restaurant aujourd'hui.

Luc _____ (2) faim. Quand Luc arrive chez Sophie, Sophie

n'_____ (3) pas prête. Luc _____ (4) fâché.

LUC: Sophie! Tu _____ (5) folle?

SOPHIE: Pourquoi est-ce que tu _____ (6) tellement pressé, Luc?

Nous ne _____ (7) pas en retard.

LUC: J'_____ (8) faim et j'_____ (9) soif.

SOPHIE: Si tu _____ (10) soif, tu peux _____ (11) du jus

d'orange. Il y a du jus d'orange dans le frigo.

LUC: Tu _____ (12) raison. Il n'_____ (13) pas tard.

SOPHIE: Est-ce qu'il _____ (14) chaud dehors?

LUC: Non, il _____ (15) assez frais et je crois qu'il

_____ (16) pleuvoir.

SOPHIE: Alors, je _____ (17) chercher mon parapluie et on

_____ (18) descendre. Moi aussi, j'_____ (19) très

faim.

LUC: On _____ (20) un taxi?

SOPHIE: C'est une bonne idée. On arrive très vite en taxi.

J. **Composition.** Imagine you are introducing yourself to a French pen pal. Tell about yourself: your name, how old you are, who the members of your family are, what you study at school, what you do in your spare time, etc. Use expressions with **avoir** to tell how you feel after school, after playing tennis, after studying for six hours, etc.

Additional Negative Expressions; Questions with Inversion

I. Negative Words

■ Verbs are made negative in French by placing **ne** before the verb and **pas** after it.

—Je **n'ai pas** faim. Je **ne vais pas** déjeuner. Et toi?

—Moi, je **ne mange pas** le matin. Donc, j'ai très faim et je veux manger.

I'm not hungry. I'm not going to have lunch. What about you?

I don't eat in the morning. So, I'm very hungry and I want to eat.

■ Several other negative words can replace **pas.**

jamais *never*	**personne** *nobody*
plus *no more, no longer*	**rien** *nothing*

—Jacques **n'est jamais** là.

—C'est qu'il **ne travaille plus** ici.

*Jacques **is never** here.*

*That's because he **doesn't work** here **anymore.***

—Je **n'achète rien** au marché aujourd'hui.

—Vous **n'invitez personne**, alors?

*I'm **not buying anything** at the market today.*

*So you're **not inviting anyone** (over) then?*

■ The indefinite article and the partitive article change to **de** after **pas, plus,** and **jamais.**

Les enfants **ne mangent plus de** bonbons.

Je **ne prends jamais de** vin.

*The children **are not eating any more** candy.*

*I **never drink** wine.*

■ Study the following pairs of affirmative words and their negative equivalents.

encore *still*	/	**plus** *no more, anymore*
quelquefois *sometimes*	/	**jamais** *never*
toujours *always*	/	**jamais** *never*
souvent *often*	/	**jamais** *never*
quelqu'un *somebody, someone*	/	**personne** *nobody, no one*
quelque chose *something*	/	**rien** *nothing*

A. Tout change. Martine is back in her neighborhood after a year in France on an exchange program. She asks if things are still the same. Tell her they are not any longer using **ne... plus.**

Modèle   —Les Durand habitent encore ici?
➢   —Non, ils n'habitent plus ici.

1. —Toi, tu joues encore au volley-ball?

_____

2. —Christine fait encore de la natation?

_____

3. —Elvire et Marguerite font encore du français?

_____

4. —Le professeur de physique est encore fâché contre toi?

_____

5. —Sylvie veut encore étudier en Europe?

_____

6. —Mme Jonquières enseigne encore au lycée?

_____

7. —Charles et toi, vous allez encore au cinéma le samedi?

_____

8. —Serge travaille encore au magasin de vêtements?

_____

B. Un fils difficile. Mme Leboucher is having difficulty with her son Marcel. She complains of the things he never does. Write what she says using the phrases indicated and **ne... jamais.**

Modèle   être à l'heure
➢   Il n'est jamais à l'heure.

1. ranger ses affaires

_____

2. faire ses devoirs

_____

3. prendre le petit déjeuner

_____

4. faire son lit

_____

5. travailler

_____

6. répondre aux questions du professeur

_____

7. être poli

_____

8. avoir honte

_____

C. Rien. You and the other students are not happy with this particular class. Answer the principal's questions with **ne... rien** to tell him what's wrong.

Modèle —Est-ce que vous apprenez quelque chose?
➤ —Non, nous n'apprenons rien.

1. —Est-ce que vous écrivez quelque chose?

— _____

2. —Est-ce que vous étudiez quelque chose?

— _____

3. —Est-ce que vous comprenez quelque chose?

— _____

4. —Est-ce que vous faites quelque chose?

— _____

5. —Est-ce que vous rédigez _(are you writing)_ quelque chose?

— _____

➤➤➤➤➤

6. —Est-ce que vous finissez quelque chose?

   — _____

7. —Est-ce que vous recopiez quelque chose?

   — _____

8. —Est-ce que vous révisez *(are you reviewing)* quelque chose?

   — _____

D. Pour avoir des amis. Use **ne... personne** and the verbs indicated to describe an annoying student *(fem.)* and a pleasant student *(fem.)*.

Modèle   L'élève pénible (écouter)
➤ Elle n'écoute personne.

L'élève pénible

1. saluer   _____

2. inviter   _____

3. aimer   _____

4. comprendre   _____

L'élève sympathique

5. déranger   _____

6. ennuyer   _____

7. imiter   _____

8. détester   _____

II. Questions with Inversion

■ You have already reviewed two ways to turn a statement into a question.

   1. Add a question mark to the statement without making any other changes.

      Vous faites du jogging tous les   *Do you jog every day?*
      jours?

2. Add the phrase **est-ce que** to the beginning of the statement.

> **Est-ce que** vous faites du jogging tous les jours? *Do you jog every day?*

■ In written French and in formal spoken French there is a third way to ask a question. The subject pronoun is placed after the verb and connected to it by a hyphen. This is called *inversion*.

> **Faites-vous** du jogging tous les jours? *Do you go jogging every day?*

■ When the third-person singular pronouns **il, elle,** and **on** are inverted, they are always preceded by the sound /t/. If the verb form does not already end in **t** or **d,** then -**t**- is added in writing.

> **Parle-t-il** français? *Does he speak French?*
>
> Où **va-t-elle?** *Where is she going?*
>
> Quand **déjeune-t-on?** *When is lunch time?*
>
> Y **a-t-il** un cinéma près d'ici? *Is there a movie theater near here?*

■ Compare verb forms of the -**ir** and -**re** verbs and irregular verbs where the addition of -**t**- is not necessary.

> Que **choisit-il?** *What is he choosing?*
>
> **Comprend-elle** l'allemand? *Does she understand German?*

■ When the subject of the sentence is a noun, the noun is not inverted. Instead, the corresponding subject pronoun (**il, elle, ils, elles**) is placed after the verb and the noun subject remains in its position before the verb.

> **Jean parle-t-il** français? *Does John speak French?*
>
> **Marie va-t-elle** au théâtre? *Is Marie going to the theater?*
>
> **Ces étudiants sont-ils** travailleurs? *Are these students hard-working?*
>
> **Vos sœurs font-elles** des langues? *Are your sisters studying languages?*
>
> **Cet enfant a-t-il** peur des chiens? *Is this child afraid of dogs?*

■ To form a negative question using inversion, **ne** is placed before the verb and **pas** or any other negative word after the inverted subject pronoun.

> **Jean ne parle-t-il pas** français? *Doesn't John speak French?*
>
> **N'allez-vous plus** au cinéma? *Don't you go to the movies anymore?*
>
> Marie **n'essaie-t-elle** jamais de comprendre? *Doesn't Marie ever try to understand?*

■ Inversion is *not* used with the pronoun **je.**

> **Est-ce que** j'ai le bon numéro? *Do I have the right number?*

E. **Interview.** M. Lamoureux is the personnel manager for a small company. He's interviewing a job applicant. Write out the questions he would ask her using **vous** and inversion. Not all questions will have question words.

Modèle   comment/trouver notre entreprise
➤ Comment trouvez-vous notre entreprise?

Les affaires (business)	
l'entreprise *(fem.)* firm, company	le produit *product*
l'expérience *(fem.) experience*	

1. arriver toujours à l'heure

   _____

2. parler anglais

   _____

3. comprendre l'allemand

   _____

4. pourquoi/vouloir travailler ici

   _____

5. aimer voyager

   _____

6. être patiente et travailleuse

   _____

7. avoir de l'expérience avec nos produits

   _____

8. quand/pouvoir commencer

   _____

F. Un nouveau lycée. Here are some questions that Janine has about her new school. Rephrase them using inversion so that they could be written in a formal letter.

Modèle   Le lycée est grand?
         ➤ Le lycée est-il grand?

Le lycée

l'activité *(fem.)* **parascolaire**
extracurricular activity

la cabine *booth (language lab)*

la permanence *study hall,*
study room

le voyage scolaire *school trip*

aider *to help*

rester ouvert *to remain open*

fermé *closed*

ouvert *open*

à toute heure *at any time*

pendant *during*

---

1. La bibliothèque reste ouverte pendant le week-end?

_____

2. Les professeurs aident leurs étudiants?

_____

3. Il y a des permanences ouvertes à toute heure?

_____

4. Combien de cabines est-ce que vous avez au laboratoire de langues?

_____

5. Est-ce qu'on organise des activités parascolaires?

_____

6. Est-ce que les classes commencent en automne?

_____

7. Est-ce qu'on fait des voyages scolaires en été?

_____

8. Est-ce qu'on emploie des ordinateurs pour rédiger?

_____

Le lycée

- The **lycée** in France follows the **collège** and students study there for three years.
- The years are called **seconde, première,** and **terminale,** in that order.
- Students in **seconde** take mostly the same subjects (French, math, life and earth science, history-geography, foreign language and physical education plus two electives).
- In **première** students choose one of three areas of concentration (called **filières**): language and literature, economics and social sciences, or science. Although most of the courses are the same for all students (French, philosophy, history and geography, etc.), students choose advanced work in their area in addition to the core of courses.
- A diploma (**baccalauréat**) is awarded after students pass a rigorous national oral and written exam in all subjects. The exam is not administered by the students' own teachers, but at assigned central testing locations.

G. Composition. Write four sentences telling what you and your friends never do at school. Use the **nous** form of the verb.

Irregular -ir Verbs

I. *-Ir* Verbs Conjugated Like *-er* Verbs

■ A small number of **-ir** verbs are conjugated like **-er** verbs.

OUVRIR *TO OPEN*

singular	**plural**
j'ouvr**e**	nous ouvr**ons**
tu ouvr**es**	vous ouvr**ez**
il/elle/on ouvr**e**	ils/elles ouvr**ent**

The verbs **couvrir** *(to cover)* and **découvrir** *(to discover)* are conjugated like **ouvrir.**

■ The verb **offrir** is also conjugated like an **-er** verb.

OFFRIR *TO OFFER*

singular	**plural**
j'offr**e**	nous offr**ons**
tu offr**es**	vous offr**ez**
il/elle/on offr**e**	ils/elles offr**ent**

Offrir also means *to give something as a gift.*

—Qu'est-ce tu **offres** à tes amis
pour leur anniversaire?

—J'**offre** toujours des livres à mes
amis.

What (gifts) **do** *you* **give** *your friends
for their birthday?*

I always **give** *my friends books
(as a gift).*

A. **Qu'est-ce qu'on ouvre?** Use the verb **ouvrir** to tell what each person is opening. Use stressed pronouns where indicated.

Modèle   l'avocat/son agenda
➤ L'avocat ouvre son agenda.

1. les secrétaires/les bureaux _____

2. le professeur/la porte   _____

3. moi/les fenêtres   _____

4. toi/ton journal   _____

5. les enfants/leurs cadeaux   _____

6. les étudiants/les tiroirs _____

7. vous/la boîte de bonbons _____

8. nous/nos lettres _____

B. Les jeunes détectives. A group of friends is trying to find out why some people in their neighborhood are behaving suspiciously. Use the verb **découvrir** to tell what they discover. Use stressed pronouns where possible.

Modèle François/comment ils s'appellent
➤ François découvre comment ils s'appellent.

1. vous/où ils habitent

_____

2. moi/pourquoi ils restent toujours chez eux

_____

3. Catherine et Paulette/comment ils travaillent

_____

4. toi/quand ils descendent

_____

5. Julie et Thomas/combien d'argent ils ont

_____

6. Gérard/comment ils écoutent nos conversations

_____

7. nous/qui travaille avec eux

_____

8. leur voisin/à qui ils envoient des lettres

_____

C. Oh, les beaux cadeaux! Tell what gifts people are giving and getting using the verb **offrir.**

Modèle   Luc/fleurs/son amie Suzanne
        ➤ Luc offre des fleurs à son amie Suzanne.

Des cadeaux

l'atlas (*masc.*) du monde *world atlas*   le foulard (*silk*) *scarf*

le ballon de football *soccer ball*   le logiciel *software package*

la cravate *necktie*   la montre *watch*

la fleur *flower*

---

1. Renée/bonbons/professeur

    _____

2. nous/atlas du monde/notre ami Maurice

    _____

3. mes parents/montre/ma sœur

    _____

4. tu/logiciel/tes cousins

    _____

5. je/ballon de football/mon petit frère

    _____

6. vous/cravate/Robert

    _____

7. Paulette/disques compacts/Martin

    _____

8. Philippe/foulard/Michèle

    _____

II. -Ir Verbs Conjugated Like -re Verbs

■ Some common -ir verbs are conjugated like -re verbs. Study the conjugation of **partir** (to leave, set out).

PARTIR TO LEAVE, SET OUT

singular	plural
je pars	nous part**ons**
tu pars	vous part**ez**
il/elle/on par**t**	ils/elles part**ent**

■ These verbs lose the final consonant of the stem in the singular (the **t** of **part-**). Compare the conjugations of the following verbs.

SORTIR TO GO OUT (STEM: SORT-)

singular	plural
je sors	nous sort**ons**
tu sors	vous sort**ez**
il/elle/on sor**t**	ils/elles sort**ent**

DORMIR TO SLEEP (STEM: DORM-)

singular	plural
je dors	nous dorm**ons**
tu dors	vous dorm**ez**
il/elle/on dor**t**	ils/elles dorm**ent**

MENTIR TO LIE (STEM: MENT-)

singular	plural
je mens	nous ment**ons**
tu mens	vous ment**ez**
il/elle/on men**t**	ils/elles ment**ent**

SERVIR TO SERVE (STEM: SERV-)

singular	plural
je sers	nous serv**ons**
tu sers	vous serv**ez**
il/elle/on ser**t**	ils/elles serv**ent**

D. On part! Say in each case that the person mentioned is not staying, but leaving.

Modèle Jacques
➢ Jacques ne reste pas. Il part.

1. tu _____

2. les étudiants _____

3. le médecin _____

4. nous _____

5. on _____

6. vous _____

7. Élisabeth _____

8. je _____

E. Demain, les vacances! Everyone asked about vacation plans is leaving tomorrow. Say so by answering with **partir.**

Modèle   —Anne-Marie va en vacances?
   ➤ —Oui, elle part demain.

1. —Tu vas en vacances?

   — _____

2. —Tes parents vont en vacances?

   — _____

3. —Tes amis et toi, vous allez en vacances?

   — _____

4. —Je vais en vacances?

   — _____

5. —Jean-Luc va en vacances?

   — _____

6. —Ma sœur et moi, nous allons en vacances?

   — _____

7. —On va en vacances? *(answer with* **on***)*

   — _____

8. —Rose et Vivienne vont en vacances?

   — _____

F. Tout le monde sort. No one is staying home this evening. Everyone is going out. Write exchanges saying so using the verb **rester** *(to remain),* the preposition **chez,** and the verb **sortir.**

Modèle   Jacques ➤
         —Jacques reste chez lui ce soir?
         —Non, il sort.

1. tes cousins

    —_____

    —_____

2. tu

    —_____

    —_____

3. je

    —_____

    —_____

4. Georges et son frère

    —_____

    —_____

5. ta cousine Zoé

    —_____

    —_____

6. Paul et moi

    —_____

    —_____

7. ton frère et toi

    —_____

    —_____

8. on *(answer with* **on***)*

    —_____

    —_____

G. Une pleine maisonnée *(A houseful of people)*. The Chaillot family has a houseful of guests. Pierre Chaillot tells where each one is sleeping. Write what he says using the verb **dormir**. Use stressed pronouns where indicated.

Modèle   mes parents/dans leur chambre
    ➤ Mes parents dorment dans leur chambre.

1. moi/dans mon lit

    _____

2. mon cousin Jérôme/dans un sac de couchage

    _____

3. Jérôme et moi/dans ma chambre

    _____

4. mon oncle et ma tante/dans la chambre d'amis

    _____

5. notre ami Nicolas/sur un lit de camp dans la salle à manger

    _____

6. ma cousine Éloïse/sur le canapé dans la salle de séjour

    _____

7. toi, Gérard/sur un lit de camp dans la cuisine

    _____

8. notre chat/dans la salle de bains

    _____

H. Les braves gens *(Decent people)*. These fine people never lie. Say so using the verb **mentir** and **ne... jamais**. Don't use stressed pronouns in this exercise.

Modèle   mon père
    ➤ Mon père ne ment jamais.

1. tu   _____

2. mon amie Claudette   _____ _____

3. mes parents   _____

➤➤➤➤➤

4. vous   _____

5. nous   _____

6. Luc et Marc   _____

7. je   _____

8. mes sœurs   _____

I. Servir à boire. Say what these people offer their guests to drink using the verb **servir** and the partitive article. Use stressed pronouns where indicated.

Modèle   ma tante/jus d'orange
➤ Ma tante sert du jus d'orange.

1. toi/bière   _____

2. ma grand-mère/limonade _____

3. mes parents/café   _____

4. vous/thé   _____

5. mon oncle/vin   _____

6. nous/gazeux   _____

7. à la cantine, on/lait   _____

8. moi/eau   _____

J. Les vacances de Sophie. Complete the following account of Sophie's vacation with the correct forms of the verbs in parentheses.

Sophie est en vacances. Elle _____ (1. partir) pour la Côte avec

sa famille. Il _____ (2. faire) beau sur la Côte. Sophie et ses parents

_____ (3. sortir) tous les jours. Sophie _____ (4. découvrir) un

nouveau monde. Les plages sont magnifiques. Dans les restaurants on

_____ (5. servir) des repas délicieux. Sophie et ses parents _____

(6. découvrir) des petits villages charmants. Sophie _____ (7. dormir)

bien parce qu'il ne fait pas trop chaud la nuit. Il y a très peu de bruit *(noise)*.

On _____ (8. entendre) la mer et les mouettes *(seagulls)*, c'est tout.

La Côte

- **La Côte** refers to **La Côte d'Azur** or the French Riviera, the Mediterranean coast of France with such famous resort areas as **Nice, Cannes, St-Tropez, Antibes,** and the independent principality **Monaco.**
- The area offers many other attractions such as the beautiful university town of **Aix-en-Provence** and the superbly preserved Roman amphitheatre and **Maison Carrée** of **Nîmes.** The beautiful scenery of **Provence** (the region in which the Côte d'Azur is located) has inspired many artists such as the French painter **Cézanne** and the Dutch painter **Van Gogh.** The cuisine of the Côte d'Azur and Provence is also famous. **Bouillabaisse** (the fish and seafood soup of Marseille), **cassoulet** (a stew), **ratatouille** (an eggplant and vegetable stew), and **aioli** (a rich garlic mayonnaise eaten with vegetables) are favorites with French people and foreigners alike.

K. Questions personnelles. Answer the following questions in French.

1. Votre famille et vous, quand partez-vous en vacances cette année?

_____

2. Est-ce que les étudiants ouvrent leurs livres dans la classe de français?

_____

3. Qu'est-ce que vous servez quand vos amis viennent vous voir chez vous?

_____

4. Est-ce que vous sortez en semaine ou seulement pendant le week-end?

_____

5. Est-ce que vous aimez les gens qui mentent?

_____

6. Est-ce que vous dormez bien quand vous avez des examens?

_____

Mettre; Quel; Savoir and connaître

I. *Mettre*

■ The verb **mettre** *(to put)* is irregular.

METTRE *TO PUT*

singular	plural
je **mets**	nous **mettons**
tu **mets**	vous **mettez**
il/elle/on **met**	ils/elles **mettent**

A. Nous rangeons nos affaires. The students and the teacher are straightening up the classroom. Write where each one is putting the things lying about using the verb **mettre,** the prepositions, and the places given. Use stressed pronouns where indicated.

Modèle   le professeur/dictionnaire/sur/la table
➢ Le professeur met le dictionnaire sur la table.

Les affaires

le dossier *file*	**la serviette** *briefcase*
le fichier *filing cabinet*	**le surligneur** *highlighter*
le placard *closet*	**le trombone** *paper clip*
le pupitre *student's desk*	

---

1. Maurice et Lise/livres/sur/l'étagère

   _____

2. nous/les examens/sur/le bureau du professeur

   _____

3. le professeur/les examens/dans/sa serviette

   _____

4. moi/dossiers/dans/le fichier

   _____

5. les étudiants/les cahiers d'exercices/dans/leurs pupitres

_____

6. toi/trombones/dans/le tiroir

_____

7. vous/surligneurs/dans/le placard

_____

8. Sylvie/logiciels/à côté de/l'ordinateur

_____

B. **Quel froid!** Say what each person is putting on to go out on this freezing winter day. Use the verb **mettre** (which also means _to put on an article of clothing_) and the appropriate possessive adjective. Use stressed pronouns where indicated.

Modèle Laurent/anorak
➤ Laurent met son anorak.

Quoi mettre en hiver?	
l'anorak _(masc.) parka_	**les gants** _(masc. pl.) gloves_
le blouson _windbreaker_	**le manteau** _coat_
le bonnet _woolen cap_	**le pantalon** _pants_
les bottes _(fem.) boots_	**le pull** _sweater_
l'écharpe _(fem.) scarf_	

1. Suzanne et Christine/bottes

_____

2. toi/pull

_____

3. Hélène/écharpe

_____

4. moi/blouson

_____

➤➤➤➤➤

5. nous/manteaux

_____

6. vous/bonnets

_____

7. ma petite sœur/pantalon en laine

_____

8. Jacques et Louis/gants

_____

C. Il fait chaud aujourd'hui. A group of friends is going out in Nice on a hot summer day. Each one is putting on something comfortable for summer. Use the verb **mettre** and the appropriate possessive adjective to tell what each friend is wearing. Use stressed pronouns where indicated.

Modèle   Albert/jean
   ➤ Albert met son jean.

1. Lucie/chapeau

_____

2. Vincent et Georges/baskets *(sneakers)*

_____

3. moi/short

_____

4. toi/tee-shirt

_____

5. nous/sandales

_____

6. vous/lunettes de soleil

_____

7. Serge/maillot de bain

_____

8. Julie et Claudine/bikinis

_____

II. Quel?

■ **Quel** is an interrogative adjective meaning *which?* It has four forms.

Quel pull vas-tu offrir?	*Which sweater are you going to give (as a gift)?*
Quelle robe veux-tu essayer?	*Which dress do you want to try on?*
Quels gants vas-tu choisir?	*Which gloves are you going to choose?*
Quelles chaussures veux-tu acheter?	*Which shoes do you want to buy?*

■ **Quel** + *the noun* that follows it, like other question words, can come at the end of the sentence also. When the interrogative word is at the end of the sentence, there is no inversion.

Tu veux acheter **quelles chaussures?**	*Which shoes do you want to buy?*
Le train arrive **à quelle heure?**	*At what time does the train arrive?*
Tu sors **avec qui?**	*Whom are you going out with?*
Marcelle travaille **où?**	*Where does Marcelle work?*
Nous partons **quand?**	*When do we leave?*
Ça fait **combien?**	*How much does it cost?*

■ **Quel** is also used before nouns in exclamations.

Quel hiver!	*What a winter!*
Quels vêtements!	*What clothing!*

D. **Au magasin de vêtements.** Mireille and Alice are looking at items in a clothing store. One says what she likes; the other asks which item she means. Use demonstrative adjectives and **quel?** to write out what they say to each other.

Modèle chemisier ➤
    —J'aime ce chemisier.
    —Quel chemisier?

1. bas

— _____   — _____

2. robe

— _____   — _____

➤➤➤➤➤

3. chaussures

—_____   —_____

4. collants

—_____   —_____

5. bonnet

—_____   —_____

6. sandales

—_____   —_____

7. ceinture

—_____   —_____

8. imperméable

—_____   —_____

E. Des doutes. Francine is concerned about her clothing. She wonders in each case what she should do. Write out her thoughts using the interrogative adjective **quel?** and the verb **devoir.**

Modèle   robe/porter
➤ Quelle robe est-ce que je dois porter?

Des verbes pour les vêtements	
acheter *to buy*	**mettre** *to put on*
choisir *to choose*	**offrir** *to give (as a gift)*
essayer *to try on*	**porter** *to wear*

1. chaussettes/mettre

_____

2. foulard/offrir à Louise

_____

3. collants/choisir

_____

4. gants/essayer

_____

5. cravate/offrir à mon frère

_____

6. boucles d'oreille/acheter

_____

7. chapeau/mettre

_____

8. jupe/porter

_____

F. Une jeune ménage *(Married couple)*. Stéphane and Valérie are discussing what they are going to wear. Use the interrogative adjective, the verb **mettre,** a possessive adjective, and the adjectives of color to write out what they say.

Modèle   jupe/rouge ➤
   STÉPHANE: —Tu vas mettre quelle jupe aujourd'hui?
   VALÉRIE: —Aujourd'hui je mets ma jupe rouge.

Note: The words **orange** and **marron** are invariable. They do not change to show gender and number agreement.

1. baskets/bleu

   V: — _____

   S: — _____

2. chaussures/marron

   S: — _____

   V: — _____

3. veste/gris

   V: — _____

   S: — _____

➤➤➤➤➤

4. foulard/orange

S: — _____

V: — _____

5. chemise/blanc

V: — _____

S: — _____

6. chaussettes/jaune

S: — _____

V: — _____

7. cravate/beige et vert

V: — _____

S: — _____

8. manteau/rouge et noir

S: — _____

V: — _____

III. *Savoir* and *connaître*

■ The verbs **savoir** and **connaître** mean *to know*. They are irregular.

SAVOIR

singular	plural
je **sais**	nous **savons**
tu **sais**	vous **savez**
il/elle/on **sait**	ils/elles **savent**

CONNAÎTRE

singular	plural
je **connais**	nous **connaissons**
tu **connais**	vous **connaissez**
il/elle/on **connaît**	ils/elles **connaissent**

Note the circumflex accent on the **i** in **il connaît**.

■ Although both **savoir** and **connaître** mean *to know*, they are not interchangeable. **Savoir** means *to know facts or information*. It is not used before names of people.

—Tu **sais** le nom de cette fille?	*Do you **know** that girl's name?*
—Oui, elle s'appelle Sylvie.	*Yes, her name is Sylvie.*
—Tu **sais** son adresse?	*Do you **know** her address?*
—Oui, mais je ne **sais** pas son téléphone.	*Yes, but I don't **know** her phone number.*

■ **Savoir** may have a noun as its object, as in the above examples (**le nom, l'adresse, le téléphone**) or a sentence. The sentence object is called a subordinate clause.

—Tu **sais** où Christophe travaille?	*Do you **know** where Christophe works?*
—Non, mais je **sais** qu'il travaille en ville.	*No, but I **know** that he works downtown.*

The subordinate clauses are **où Christophe travaille** and **qu'il travaille en ville.**

■ The verb **connaître** means *to know or be familiar with people or places*. It is always followed by a noun and is not followed by subordinate clauses.

—Je **connais** Mme Verdier. Elle est de Lyon.	*I **know** Madame Verdier. She is from Lyon.*
—Tu **connais** Lyon?	*Do you **know** Lyons? (= Have you ever been to Lyons?)*

G. Que savez-vous? Complete the following conversations with the correct forms of **savoir** or **connaître.**

a. —Qui est ce garçon?

—Je ne _____ (1) pas. Je ne _____ (2) pas ce garçon.

—On va demander à Christine. Elle _____ (3) tout le monde.

Christine!

—Oui?

—Qui est ce garçon?

—Je _____ (4) que c'est un nouvel étudiant, mais je ne

_____ (5) pas comment il s'appelle.

b. —Pardon, monsieur. Où est le stade?

—Je ne _____ (6) pas exactement. Je ne _____ ___ (7) pas

cette ville. Je ne suis pas d'ici.

>>>>>

c. —Tu _____ (8) si Jean-Marc _____ (9) bien Montréal?

—Sans doute. Je _____ (10) que sa famille va au Canada tous les

étés.

—Ils aiment bien le Canada, je suppose.

—Oui, ils _____ (11) beaucoup de Canadiens.

d. —Vous _____ (12) quelqu'un à Paris?

—Non, je ne _____ (13) personne dans cette ville.

—Vous _____ (14) que j'ai une cousine qui habite Paris? Tu veux

son téléphone?

—Bien sûr. Est-elle née à Paris?

—Ah, oui. Elle _____ (15) très bien la ville.

e. —Je n'aime plus mes vêtements. Je ne _____ (16) plus quoi

mettre. J'ai besoin de nouveaux vêtements.

—Ma sœur et moi, nous _____ (17) un bon magasin de

vêtements.

—C'est où, ce magasin?

—Tu _____ (18) le quartier de Saint-Martin?

—Pas très bien, mais je _____ (19) que Julie habite ce quartier.

—Tu as raison. Si tu _____ (20) où elle habite, tu peux trouver

le magasin. Il est très près de son immeuble.

H. Vos vêtements. Describe what you wear at different times during the year and/or to different places (school, parties). What kind of clothing is now fashionable or out of fashion? Write a paragraph of five or six sentences about clothing.

Quelques expressions

être à la mode to be in fashion

être démodé to be out of fashion

Prepositions; Prepositions with Geographical Names; Adjectives of Nationality

I. Prepositions

- Some common French prepositions

à *at, to*	**de** *from, of*	**pour** *for, in order to*
après *after*	**derrière** *in back of, behind*	**sans** *without*
avant *before*	**devant** *in front of*	**sous** *under*
avec *with*	**en** *in, made of*	**sur** *on*
chez *at the house of*	**entre** *between*	
dans *in*	**jusqu'à** *until*	

- Remember that the prepositions **à** and **de** contract with the definite articles **le** and **les**.

à + le ➤ au	**de + le ➤ du**
à + les ➤ aux	**de + les ➤ des**

- The preposition **en** is used tell what something is made of.

la laine *wool*	**un pantalon en laine** *woolen pants*
le coton *cotton*	**une chemise en coton** *a cotton shirt*
le jean *denim*	**une jupe en jean** *a denim skirt*
le cuir *leather*	**une ceinture en cuir** *a leather belt*

- French also has phrases ending in **de** that serve as prepositions.

à côté de *next to*	**en face de** *opposite, across from*
au bout de *at the end of*	**loin de** *far from*
au coin de *at the corner of*	**près de** *near*
au milieu de *in the middle of*	

- The contractions **du** and **des** are used when the articles **le** and **les** follow these prepositions: **près du stade, en face des magasins.**

A. Antonymes. Find a preposition in column B that expresses the opposite idea of each preposition in column A.

A

_____ 1. avec

_____ 2. après

_____ 3. de

_____ 4. devant

_____ 5. loin de

_____ 6. au milieu de

_____ 7. sur

B

a. près de

b. sous

c. avant

d. au bout de

e. à

f. derrière

g. sans

B. Des idées apparentées. Find a preposition in column B that has a similar or related meaning to each preposition of column A.

A

_____ 1. à

_____ 2. dans

_____ 3. à côté de

_____ 4. chez

_____ 5. au bout de

_____ 6. en face de

B

a. devant

b. près de

c. au coin de

d. en

e. jusqu'à

f. à la maison de

C. Les prépositions qui manquent. Circle the letter of the preposition that correctly completes each sentence.

1. Je prends mon café _____ du lait.

   a. pour   b. avec   c. jusqu'à

2. Il y un café _____ la rue, là-bas.

   a. loin de   b. au coin de   c. de

3. Elle porte un chemisier _____ coton.

   a. en   b. au   c. avec

4. Les grands-parents de Paul vivent près d'ici. Il va souvent manger _____ eux.

   a. sans   b. chez   c. sous

5. Pour aller à l'aéroport? Tu dois prendre un taxi. C'est _____ ici.

    a. à côté d'   b. en face d'   c. loin d'

6. Les enfants ne doivent pas jouer _____ la rue. C'est dangereux.

    a. au milieu de   b. en   c. devant

II. Prepositions with Geographic Names

■ With the names of cities, French uses the preposition **à** to express location or motion towards and the preposition **de** to express *from*.

—Vous êtes **de** Paris, Madame?   *Are you **from** Paris, Ma'am?*
—Oui, je rentre **à** Paris demain.   *Yes, I'm going back **to** Paris tomorrow.*

■ With the names of countries and continents you have to know the gender of the place name. With countries and continents that are feminine, no article is used. The preposition **en** expresses location or motion towards and the preposition **de** expresses *from*.

—Les Durand vont passer les vacances **en Europe**?   *Are the Durands going to spend their vacation **in Europe**?*
—Oui, ils vont **en France** et **en Allemagne.**   *Yes, they're going **to France** and Germany.*

—Tu vas travailler **en Italie** cet été?   *Are you going to work **in Italy** this summer?*

—Non, **en Espagne.** Je fais de l'espagnol.   *No, **in Spain.** I'm studying Spanish.*

—Le nouvel étudiant est-il **de Belgique**?   *Is the new student **from Belgium**?*
—Non, je crois qu'il vient **de Suisse.**   *No, I think he comes **from Switzerland.***

■ Countries that don't end in **e** are masculine.

le Canada *Canada*

le Danemark *Denmark*

les États-Unis *(masc. pl.) United States*

les Pays-Bas *(masc. pl.) The Netherlands*

le Portugal *Portugal*

Note however that **le Mexique** *(Mexico)* is masculine.

■ With masculine countries **à** expresses location or motion towards and the preposition **de** expresses *from*. The article remains and the appropriate contractions are formed.

—Luc revient **des États-Unis** aujourd'hui?   *Is Luc coming back **from the** U.S. today?*
—Oui, mais demain il va **au Canada.**   *Yes, but tomorrow he's going **to** Canada.*

—Pedro est portugais?
—Oui, il vient **du Portugal,** mais il habite **au Mexique.**

Is Pedro Portuguese?
Yes, he comes from Portugal, but he lives in Mexico.

■ Here are the names of some former French colonies in Africa.

masculine	feminine
le Bénin *Benin (formerly Dahomey)*	**l'Algérie** *Algeria*
le Cameroun *Cameroon(s)*	**la Côte-d'Ivoire** *Ivory Coast*
le Congo *French Congo*	**la Guinée** *Guinea*
le Mali *Mali*	**la Mauritanie** *Mauritania*
le Maroc *Morocco*	**la Tunisie** *Tunisia*
le Sénégal *Senegal*	

L'Afrique francophone

As a result of French colonization in Africa, French is either the official language or the major second language of many of today's independent African nations.

■ In the three Arabic-speaking countries of North Africa—Morocco, Algeria, and Tunisia—French is widely spoken and the French press, television and radio, and French cinema are very popular. There are many North African writers from these countries who write in French.

■ In sub-Saharan Africa, French is widely used as the common language in countries where many different local languages are spoken. It is often the language of government, education, and the media in former French colonies, and French-speaking African writers have created an extraordinary literature using the French language.

D. Séjours linguistiques *(Language-learning trips abroad).* Where are these people going to practice the languages they are studying? Complete these sentences with the appropriate prepositions.

1. John et Mary font du français. Ils vont _____ France.

2. Paul fait de l'anglais. Il va _____ États-Unis.

3. Moi, je fais du portugais. Je vais _____ Portugal.

4. Toi, tu fais de l'allemand. Tu vas _____ Allemagne.

5. Barbara fait de l'espagnol. Elle va _____ Mexique.

6. Nous, nous faisons de l'arabe. Nous allons _____ Tunisie.

7. Vous, vous faites du français. Vous allez _____ Côte-d'Ivoire.

8. Carole et Justine font du néerlandais. Elles vont _____ Pays-Bas.

E. Les étudiants étrangers. Where are all these new foreign students from? Complete the following sentences with the appropriate French word for *from*.

1. Kimberley vient _____ Canada.

2. Lorenzo vient _____ Espagne.

3. Lars vient _____ Danemark.

4. Ousmane vient _____ Sénégal.

5. Laura vient _____ Italie.

6. Heidi vient _____ Suisse.

7. Mies vient _____ Pays-Bas.

8. Karima vient _____ Maroc.

F. Résidence à l'étranger. These people are not living in their countries of origin. Examine the chart below and write for each person the country he or she is from, the city that person was born in, and the country and city he or she lives in now.

Les origines

le lieu place	**le pays** country
la naissance birth	**il est né, elle est née** *he was born, she was born*
la résidence residence	

---

nom	lieu de naissance		lieu de résidence	
	pays	**ville**	**pays**	**ville**
Modèle Frédéric	France	Paris	Canada	Montréal

Frédéric vient de France. Il est né à Paris. Mais maintenant il habite au Canada, à Montréal.

1. Guy	Belgique	Bruxelles	Mexique	Mexico*
2. Fernanda	Espagne	Madrid	États-Unis	New-York
3. Marco	Italie	Rome	Angleterre	Londres
4. Hans	Allemagne	Berlin	Canada	Québec
5. Marie	Suisse	Genève	Portugal	Lisbonne
6. Ahmed	Algérie	Alger†	France	Lyon
7. Angélique	Sénégal	Dakar	Danemark	Copenhague
8. Suzie	États-Unis	Los Angeles	Côte-d'Ivoire	Abidjan

1. _____

_____

2. _____

_____

➤➤➤➤➤

---

*Le Mexique in French refers to the country Mexico. In French, Mexico City is called **Mexico**.

†**Alger** is Algiers, the capital of Algeria.

3. _____

_____

4. _____

_____

5. _____

_____

6. _____

_____

7. _____

_____

8. _____

_____

III. Adjectives of Nationality

■ Adjectives of nationality ending in -en

algérien *Algerian*	égyptien *Egyptian*	péruvien *Peruvian*
canadien *Canadian*	européen *European*	tunisien *Tunisian*
chilien *Chilean*	israélien *Israeli*	vénézuélien *Venezuelan*
colombien *Colombian*	italien *Italian*	
coréen *Korean*	norvégien *Norwegian*	

■ Other common adjectives of nationality

africain *African*	écossais *Scottish*	mexicain *Mexican*
allemand *German*	espagnol *Spanish*	néerlandais *Dutch*
américain *American*	français *French*	portugais *Portuguese*
anglais *English*	irlandais *Irish*	suédois *Swedish*
chinois *Chinese*	japonais *Japanese*	
danois *Danish*	marocain *Moroccan*	

■ The following adjectives of nationality have no separate feminine form because they end in **-e** in the masculine singular.

arabe *Arab*   **britannique** *British*   **suisse** *Swiss*

belge *Belgian*   **russe** *Russian*

G. Elle(s) aussi. Say in each case that the women mentioned are of the same nationality as the men.

Modèle   Lucien est français. (Sylvie)
              ➤ Sylvie est française aussi.

1. Pedro est mexicain. (Alicia)

   _____

2. Hideo et Kazuo sont japonais. (Yoko et Akiko)

   _____

3. David est israélien. (Rachelle et Sarah)

   _____

4. Tsche-Hong est chinois. (Shu-Ling)

   _____

5. Olivier est belge. (Marga et Katie)

   _____

6. Lars et Anders sont danois. (Lisbet)

   _____

7. Micha est russe. (Olga et Macha)

   _____

8. Abdoul et Hassan sont algériens. (Karima)

   _____

H. Composition. Write about a real or imaginary trip abroad that you are going to take. Tell how you are traveling, where you are leaving from, where you are going to, and whom you are going to see in the places you will visit. Write five or six sentences.

END VOCABULARY: FRENCH-ENGLISH

This vocabulary list contains all words used in the exercises and introduced in the vocabulary boxes. Conjugation reminders are given for verbs with spelling changes. A note such as **nager** (**g ≻ ge/a,o**) should be read as "**g** changes to **ge** before **a** and **o**." Irregular forms are indicated in parentheses. Regular adjectives are listed in the masculine singular form.

à at, to
à côté de next to
à l'heure on time, punctually
à peu près approximately
à pied on foot
à toute heure at any time
aboyer (**y ≻ i/mute e**) to bark
absolument absolutely
accompagner to accompany, go with
l' **accordéon** (*masc.*) accordion
acheter (**j'achète**) to buy
l' **activité** (*fem.*) **parascolaire** extracurricular activity
actuel (*fem.* **actuelle**) present, present-day
admirer to admire
adorer to love
l' **aéroport** (*masc.*) airport
l' **affaire** (*fem.*) matter; **les affaires** business; belongings
l' **affiche** (*fem.*) poster
africain African
l' **agenda** (*masc.*) appointment book
l' **agneau** (*masc.*) lamb
l' **agriculteur** (**l'agricultrice**) farmer
l' **agronomie** (*fem.*) agronomy, agricultural science
aider to help
aimer to like, to love
l' **album** (*masc.*) (**de bandes dessinées**) comic book
l' **algèbre** (*fem.*) algebra
l' **Algérie** (*fem.*) Algeria
algérien(ne) Algerian
les **aliments** (*masc. pl.*) food
allemand German; **l'allemand** (*masc.*) German (*language*)
aller (*irreg., passé composé with* **être**) to go; **aller (bien) à quelqu'un** to look nice on someone
alors then
l' **alto** (*masc.*) viola
américain American
l' **ami** (*masc.*) friend (*male*)
l' **amie** (*fem.*) friend (*female*)
amusant amusing, funny
l' **ananas** (*masc.*) pineapple
anglais English; **l'anglais** (*masc.*) English (*language*)
l' **animal** (*masc.; pl.* **les animaux**) animal
l' **année** (*fem.*) year

l' **anniversaire** (*masc.*) birthday
annoncer (**c ≻ ç/a,o**) to announce
l' **anorak** (*masc.*) parka
août August; **en août** in August
l' **appareil électroménager** (*masc.*) household appliance
l' **appareil-photo** (*masc.*) (still) camera
l' **appartement** (*masc.*) apartment
appeler (**j'appelle**) to call
applaudir to applaud
apporter to bring
apprendre (*irreg.*) to learn; **apprendre par cœur** to memorize
appuyer (sur) (**y ≻ i/mute e**) to press
après after, afterwards
après-demain the day after tomorrow
l' **après-midi** (*masc.*) afternoon
arabe Arab
l' **argent** money
l' **arrêt** (*masc.*) **de l'autobus** bus stop
l' **arrière-grand-mère** (*fem.*) great-grandmother
l' **arrière-grand-père** (*masc.*) great-grandfather
arriver (*passé composé with* **être**) to arrive
assez de enough
l' **atlas** (*masc.*) (**du monde**) (world) atlas
attendre to wait for
attentivement attentively
au bout de at the end of
au coin de at the corner of
au milieu de in the middle of
aujourd'hui today
autant de as much, as many
l' **autobus** (*masc.*) city bus
l' **autocar** (*masc.*) intercity bus
l' **automne** (*masc.*) fall; **en automne** in the fall
autre other
autrefois formerly, in the past
avant before, previously, beforehand
avant-hier the day before yesterday
l' **avion** (*masc.*) airplane
l' **avocat; l'avocate** lawyer
avoir (*irreg.*) to have
avoir besoin de to need
avoir chaud to be warm
avoir de la chance to be lucky
avoir envie de to feel like

avoir **faim** to be hungry
avoir **froid** to be cold
avoir **honte (de)** to be ashamed (of)
avoir **peur** to be afraid
avoir **raison** to be right
avoir **soif** to be thirsty
avoir **sommeil** to be sleepy
avoir **tort** to be wrong
avril April; **en avril** in April

le **baladeur** walkman
la **balle** ball (*smaller than a soccer ball*)
le **ballon de football** soccer ball
la **banane** banana
les **bandes dessinées** (*fem. pl.*) comics, comic strips
bas (*fem.* **basse**) low
les **bas** (*masc. pl.*) stockings
le **basket-ball** basketball
les **baskets** (*masc. pl.*) sneakers
le **bateau** (*pl.* **bateaux**) boat
le **bâtiment** building
bavarder to chat, converse, talk
beau (**bel, belle, beaux**) beautiful
beaucoup de much, many, a lot of
beige beige
le **bêlement** bleat, bleating
belge Belgian
le **Bénin** Benin (*formerly Dahomey*)
le **berger** shepherd, la **bergère** shepherdess
bête silly, stupid
la **bêtise** foolish thing
le **beurre** butter
la **bibliothèque** library
la **bicyclette** bicycle
bien well
bientôt soon
la **bière** beer
le **bikini** bikini
le **billet** ticket
la **biologie** biology
blanc (*fem.* **blanche**) white
le **blé** wheat
bleu blue
le **blouson** windbreaker
le **bœuf** beef; ox
boire (*irreg.*) to drink
la **boisson** drink
la **boîte** box; **la boîte en carton** carton; **une boîte de** a box of
bon (*fem.* **bonne**) good
les **bonbons** (*masc. pl.*) candy
le **bonnet** woolen cap
le **bosquet** grove (*of trees*)
les **bottes** (*fem. pl.*) boots
les **boucles** (*fem. pl.*) **d'oreille** earrings
la **boulette de viande** meatball
la **boum** party
la **bouteille** bottle; **une bouteille de** a bottle of
le **bouton** button
britannique British
brûler to burn
le **bureau** desk; office

ça: C'est pour ça que that's why
la **cabine** booth (*language lab*)
le **cabinet de travail** study
le **cadeau** gift
le **café** coffee; café; **le café glacé** iced coffee
le **cahier d'exercices** workbook
la **calculatrice** calculator
le **camarade** (la **camarade**) **de classe** classmate
la **caméra** camcorder, movie camera
le **Cameroun** Cameroon(s)
le **camion** truck
la **campagne** country, countryside; **à la campagne** in the country
le **Canada** Canada
canadien(ne) Canadian
le **canapé** couch, sofa
la **cantine** lunchroom
la **car** bus
la **carafe** (water) pitcher
la **carotte** carrot
carré square
la **carte** map
la **carte de Noël** Christmas card
la **carte postale** postcard
la **cassette** cassette, tape
ce (*masc. sing.*) this, that
la **ceinture** belt
célébrer (**je célèbre**) to celebrate
cent one hundred
le **centre** city center, downtown; **le centre commercial** shopping center, shopping mall
le **centre-ville** downtown
les **céréales** (*fem. pl.*) cereal
ces these, those
cet (*masc. sing. before a vowel*) this, that
cette (*fem. sing.*) this, that
la **chaîne-stéréo** stereo
la **chaise** chair
la **chambre** room; bedroom; **la chambre d'amis** guest room
le **champ** field
changer (g ≻ ge/a,o) to change
la **chanson** song
chanter to sing
le **chapeau** hat
chaque each; **chaque jour** each/every day; **chaque semaine** each/every week
charmant charming
chasser to drive, herd
le **chat** cat
les **chaussettes** (*fem. pl.*) socks
la **chaussure** shoe
la **chemise** shirt
le **chemisier** blouse
chercher to look for
le **cheval** (*pl.* **les chevaux**) horse
la **chèvre** goat
chez at the house of
le **chien** dog
chilien(ne) Chilean
la **chimie** chemistry
chinois Chinese; **le chinois** Chinese (*language*)
le **chocolat** chocolate; hot chocolate

les **choses** *(fem. pl.)* things; **faire beaucoup de choses** to do a lot of things

choisir to choose

le **cinéma** movies

cinq five

cinquante fifty

le **citron** lemon; **le citron pressé** lemonade

la **clarinette** clarinet

la **classe d'anglais** English class

le **classeur** loose-leaf notebook

la **clé** key

le **client (la cliente)** customer

le **cochon** pig

le **cœur** heart; **par cœur** by heart

les **collants** *(masc. pl.)* tights, panty hose

le **collège** French junior high or middle school

colombien(ne) Colombian

Combien de? How much, how many?

le **commencement** beginning

commencer (c ≻ ç/a,o) to begin

comment how

la **composition** composition

comprendre to understand

compter to count

le **concert** concert

la **confiserie** candy store, sweet shop

la **confiture** jam

confortable comfortable

le **Congo** (French) Congo

connaître *(irreg.)* to know *(a place or person)*

le **conseil** piece of advice; **les conseils** *(masc. pl.)* advice

constamment constantly

la **constitution** constitution

content de happy with

la **conversation** conversation

le **copain (la copine)** friend, buddy

le **coq au vin** chicken braised in red wine

la **corbeille** wastebasket

coréen(ne) Korean

corriger (g ≻ ge/a,o) to correct

la **Côte-d'Ivoire** Ivory Coast

le **coton** cotton; **en coton** cotton *(adj.)*, made of cotton

le **couloir** corridor

couper to cut; **couper en cubes** to cut into squares

couramment fluently

courir *(irreg.)* to run

le **cours** course, class, class hour

les **courses** errands

court short *(not for people)*

le **cousin, la cousine** cousin

coûter to cost

la **cravate** necktie

le **crayon** pencil

la **création** creation

la **crème caramel** custard

croire *(irreg.)* to believe; **Je crois que oui.** I think so; **Je crois que non.** I don't think so

la **croisade** crusade

cruel(le) cruel

le **cube** cube, little square

le **cuir** leather; **en cuir** leather *(adj.)*, made of leather

la **cuisine** kitchen

cultiver to grow *(plants, flowers)*

la **culture physique** gym *(school subject)*

d'abord first

les **dames** *(fem. pl.)* checkers *(game)*

le **Danemark** Denmark

danois Danish

dans in

danser to dance

de from, of

décembre December; **en décembre** in December

décider de to decide (to do something)

déclarer to declare

découvrir *(irreg.)* to discover

dedans inside

dehors outside

déjà already

le **déjeuner** lunch

déjeuner to have lunch

délicieux(-se) delicious

demain tomorrow; **demain matin** tomorrow morning; **demain soir** tomorrow evening

demander to ask for

le **déménagement** move (house)

déménager (g ≻ ge/a,o) to move *(to a new house, etc.)*

demi half

démodé out of fashion

le **département** department; French administrative division

déposer to drop off, to let off

déranger (g ≻ ge/a,o) to bother, disturb

dernier *(fem. dernière)* last, final

derrière in back of, behind

descendre (*passé composé with* **être**) to go downstairs

dessiner to draw

les **dessins animés** *(masc. pl.)* cartoons *(TV)*

détester to hate

deux two

devant in front of

devenir *(irreg., passé composé with* **être**) to become

devoir *(irreg.)* should, ought, must

les **devoirs** *(masc. pl.)* homework

d'habitude usually

le **dictionnaire** dictionary

difficile hard, difficult

dimanche Sunday; **le dimanche** on Sundays

le **dîner** dinner

dîner to have dinner

dire *(irreg.)* to say, to tell

le **directeur (la directrice)** principal *(of a school)*

le **disque compact** compact disc

dix ten

dix-huit eighteen

dix-neuf nineteen

dix-sept seventeen

donc so, therefore

donner to give

dormir *(irreg.)* to sleep

le **dossier** file

doucement softly, gently
doué talented
douze twelve
dur hard

l' eau *(fem.)* water
l' écharpe *(fem.)* scarf
les échecs *(masc. pl.)* chess
l' école *(fem.)* school
écossais Scottish
écouter to listen to
écrire *(irreg.)* to write
l' écurie *(fem.)* stable
l' éducation civique *(fem.)* civics
effacer (c ≻ ç/a,o) to erase
égyptien(ne) Egyptian
l' élève *(masc. or fem.)* pupil, elementary school
    student
élever (j'élève) to raise
elle she, it
elles *(fem.)* they
embêtant boring, annoying
l' émission *(fem.)* TV program
l' empereur *(masc.)* emperor
employer (y ≻ i/mute e) to use
en in; made of
en avance early *(ahead of time)*
en bas downstairs
en face de opposite, across from
en haut upstairs
en retard late
l' enclos *(masc.)* enclosure
encore still, yet, again; encore une fois again
l' enfant *(masc. or fem.)* child
enfin at last, finally
ennuyer (y ≻ i/mute e) to bore
ennuyeux(-se) boring
énormément enormously; an awful lot, very much
enseigner to teach
ensemble together
ensuite then, afterward
entendre to hear
entre between
l' entreprise *(fem.)* firm, company
entrer (dans) (passé composé *with* être) to enter,
    come in
envoyer (y ≻ i/mute e) to send
l' équipe *(fem.)* team
l' escalier *(masc.)* stairs
espagnol Spanish; l'espagnol *(masc.)* Spanish
    (language)
essayer to try, try on; essayer + de + *infinitive*
    to try to do something
l' étage *(masc.)* floor, story
l' étagère *(fem.)* bookcase, shelving
les États-Unis *(masc. pl.)* United States
l' été *(masc.)* summer; en été in the summer
être *(irreg.)* to be
étroit narrow
l' étudiant (l'étudiante) student
étudier to study
européen(ne) European

eux *(masc.; stressed pronoun)* they
l' examen *(masc.)* test
l' expérience *(fem.)* experience; experiment
expliquer to explain

fâché (contre) angry (with)
facile easy
facilement easily
la faculté department *(at a university)*
faire *(irreg.)* to make, to do; faire + *partitive article
    + school subject* to study *(math, music, etc.)*
faire attention to pay attention
faire de l'exercice to exercise, get some exercise
faire de la barque to row, go rowing
faire de la natation to go swimming
faire de la photographie to do photography
faire de la voile to go sailing
faire des choses to do things
faire des fautes to make mistakes
faire des projets to make plans
faire des projets de voyage to make travel plans
faire du camping to go camping
faire du jogging to jog
faire du patin à glace to ice skate, to go ice-skating
faire du patin à roulettes to roller skate, to go
    roller-skating
faire du piano, du violon to take piano, violin
    lessons
faire du sport to play sports, participate in sports
faire du vélo, de la bicyclette to go bike riding
faire la cuisine to cook, to do the cooking
faire la malle to pack the trunk
faire la vaisselle to do the dishes
faire le jardin to do the gardening
faire le linge to do the laundry
faire le lit (faire les lits) to make the bed (to make
    the beds)
faire le ménage to do the housework
faire les courses to do the marketing, run the day's
    errands
faire les valises to pack *(one's bags)*
faire pousser to grow *(plants, flowers)*
faire ses devoirs to do one's homework
faire un voyage to take a trip
faire une promenade (à pied) to go for a walk
faire une promenade en voiture to go for a ride
faire une randonnée to go hiking
faire X kilomètres to cover, go X kilometers
faire: Il fait 65 degrés. It's 65 degrees (F) (out).
faire: Il fait beau. The weather's nice.
faire: Il fait chaud. It's hot, warm.
faire: Il fait du brouillard. It's foggy.
faire: Il fait du soleil. It's sunny.
faire: Il fait du vent. It's windy.
faire: Il fait frais. It's cool.
faire: Il fait froid. It's cold.
faire: Il fait gris. It's overcast.
faire: Il fait mauvais. The weather's bad.
faire: Quelle température fait-il? What's the
    temperature?
faire: Quel temps fait-il? What's the weather like?
fatigué tired

faut: **il faut** it is necessary to, one must
la **faute** mistake
le **fauteuil** armchair, easy chair
la **femme** woman; wife
la **fenêtre** window
fermé closed
la **ferme** farm
fermer to close
le **fermier (la fermière)** farmer
feutre felt-tipped pen
février February; **en février** in February
le **fichier** filing cabinet
la **fille** girl; daughter
le **film** movie, film
le **fils** son
finir to finish
la **flaque d'eau** puddle (of water)
la **flemme** *(slang)* laziness
la **fleur** flower
la **flûte** flute
fois: **une fois** once; **deux fois** twice; **trois fois** three times; **une fois par semaine** once a week
le **football** soccer
formidable terrific
fou *(fem. folle, masc. pl. fous)* crazy
le **foulard** (silk) scarf
frais *(fem. fraîche)* fresh
la **fraise** strawberry
les **fraises** *(fem. pl.)* **à la crème** strawberries with cream
français French; **le français** French *(language)*
le **frère** brother
le **frigo** refrigerator (fridge)
les **frites** *(fem. pl.)* French fried potatoes
le **fromage** cheese
le **fruit** fruit

gagner to win
les **gants** *(masc. pl.)* gloves
le **garçon** boy; waiter
garder to keep
la **gare** railway station; **la gare routière** bus terminal
le **gâteau** cake
le **gazeux** sparkling water, mineral water
le **gazon** lawn
généreux(-se) generous
les **gens** *(masc. pl.)* people
gentil *(fem. gentille)* nice, kind, friendly
gentiment in a friendly way, nicely
la **géographie** geography
la **géométrie** geometry
la **glace** ice cream; ice
le **gobelet** paper cup
le **goûter** afternoon (after school) snack
grand big, tall
la **grand-mère** grandmother
le **grand-père** grandfather
les **grands-parents** *(masc. pl.)* grandparents
le **grenier** attic
gris gray
grossir to get fat
le **groupe** group; **en groupe** as a group

la **Guinée** Guinea
la **guitare** guitar
le **gymnase** gymnasium

l' **habitant** *(masc.)* inhabitant
habiter to live *(reside)*
le ***hamburger** hamburger
les ***haricots verts** *(masc. pl.)* green beans
***haut** high, tall
l' **heure** *(fem.)* hour; clock time
heureusement happily, fortunately
heureux(-se) happy
hier yesterday
l' **histoire** *(fem.)* history, story
l' **hiver** *(masc.)* winter; **en hiver** in the winter
l' **homme** *(masc.)* man
l' **hôpital** *(masc.; pl. les hôpitaux)* hospital
les ***hors-d'œuvre** *(masc. pl.)* hors d'oeuvres, first course
l' **hôtel** *(masc.)* hotel
***huit** eight

ici here
l' **idée** *(fem.)* idea
il he, it
il faut it is necessary
il ne faut pas one shouldn't, mustn't
il y a there is, there are; **il y a** + *expression of time* ago
ils *(masc.)* they
imiter to imitate
l' **immeuble** *(masc.)* apartment house
impatient impatient
l' **imperméable** *(masc.)* raincoat
impoli impolite
important important
l' **imprimante** *(fem.)* printer
l' **informatique** *(fem.)* computer science
intelligent intelligent
intéressant interesting
inventer to invent, make up
inviter to invite
irlandais Irish
israélien(ne) Israeli
italien(ne) Italian; **l'italien** *(masc.)* Italian *(language)*

jamais never
le **jambon** ham
janvier January; **en janvier** in January
japonais Japanese; **le japonais** Japanese *(language)*
le **jardin** garden; **le jardin potager** vegetable garden
le **jardin zoologique** zoo
jaune yellow
je I
le **jean** denim *(cloth)*; **en jean** denim *(adj.)*, made of denim
le **jean, le blue-jeans** jeans

───────────

*Indicates aspirate **h,** that is, there is no elision
(**le hamburger**).

jeter to throw; **jeter quelque chose par terre** to throw something on the floor/ground

le **jeu** (*pl.* **les jeux**) game; **le jeu vidéo** video game

jeudi Thursday; **le jeudi** on Thursdays

jeune young

joli pretty

jouer to play; **jouer à** to play (*a game*); **jouer de** to play (*an instrument*)

les **jouets** (*masc. pl.*) toys

le **journal** (*pl.* **les journaux**) newspaper

la **journée** day

juillet July; **en juillet** in July

juin June; **en juin** in June

les **jumeaux** (*masc. pl.; fem. pl.* **les jumelles**) twins

la **jupe** skirt

le **jus** juice; **le jus d'orange** orange juice; **le jus de fruits** fruit juice

jusqu'à until

le **kilo** kilogram

le **kilomètre** kilometer (*⅝ of a mile*)

là-bas there, over there

le **laboratoire de langues** language laboratory

le **lac** lake

la **laine** wool; **en laine** woolen, made of wool

laisser to let, to leave; **laisser quelqu'un tranquille** to leave someone alone

le **lait** milk

la **lampe** lamp

la **langue** language; tongue

large wide

le **latin** Latin

la **leçon** lesson

le **légume** vegetable

le **lendemain** the day after, the next day

lentement slowly

la **lettre** letter

leur, leurs their

la **librairie** bookstore

libre free

la **limonade** non-cola soft drink

lire (*irreg.*) to read

lisiblement legibly

la **liste** list; **la liste de courses** shopping list

le **lit** bed; **le lit de camp** cot

le **litre** liter (*1.06 quarts*)

la **littérature** literature

le **livre** book

la **livre** pound (*measurement*)

le **logiciel** software package

loin de far from

les **loisirs** (*masc. pl.*) leisure-time activities

long (*fem.* **longue**) long

longtemps for a long time

louer to rent

lui (*stressed pronoun*) he, him

lundi Monday; **le lundi** on Mondays

les **lunettes** (*fem. pl.*) eyeglasses; **les lunettes de soleil** sunglasses

le **lycée** high school

mâcher du chewing-gum to chew gum

le **magasin** store; **le magasin de vêtements** clothing store

le **magnétophone** tape player

le **magnétoscope** VCR

mai May; **en mai** in May

maigrir to get thinner, lose weight

le **maillot de bain** bathing suit

maintenant now

le **maïs** corn

la **maisonnée** household

mal badly

malade sick

malheureux(-se) unhappy

le **Mali** Mali

la **malle** trunk (*luggage*)

la **maman** mother

manger (g ≻ ge/a,o) to eat

le **manteau** coat

le **marché** market

mardi Tuesday; **le mardi** on Tuesdays

le **Maroc** Morocco

marocain Moroccan

marron (*invariable*) brown

mars March; **en mars** in March

le **match** sports event

les **maths** (*fem. pl.*) mathematics

la **matière** (school) subject

le **matin** morning; in the morning

la **Mauritanie** Mauritania

mauvais bad

le **médecin** doctor (*male or female*)

le **mensonge** lie

mentir (*irreg.*) to lie, tell a lie

mercredi Wednesday; **le mercredi** on Wednesdays

la **mère** mother

merveilleux(-se) wonderful

le **métro** subway

mettre (*irreg.*) to put, put on; **mettre la table** to set the table

mexicain Mexican

Mexico Mexico City

le **Mexique** Mexico

midi noon

le **miel** honey

mignon(ne) cute

le **mille** mile

mille one thousand

un **million** a million

minuit midnight

la **mobylette** moped

la **mode** fashion; **être à la mode** to be in fashion

moderne modern

moi (*stressed pronoun*) I, me

moins less, minus

Mon Dieu! My gosh! (*not at all offensive in French*)

mon, ma, mes my

le **monde** world; **tout le monde** everyone

monter (*passé composé with* **être**) to go upstairs

la **montre** watch

montrer to show; **montrer quelque chose à quelqu'un** to show something to someone

le **monument** monument

le	**morpion** tic-tac-toe *(game)*		les	**passe-temps** free time

le **morpion** tic-tac-toe *(game)*
la **mort** death
le **mot** word
la **mousse au chocolat** chocolate cake
le **mouton** sheep
le **moyen de transport** means of transportation
la **moyenne** average; **en moyenne** on (an) average
le **mur** wall
mûr ripe
le **musée** museum

nager to swim
néerlandais Dutch; **le néerlandais** Dutch *(language)*
neiger to snow; **il neige** it's snowing
nettoyer to clean
neuf nine
noir black
norvégien(ne) Norwegian; **le norvégien** Norwegian *(language)*
noter to jot down, write down
les **notes** *(fem. pl.)* notes; grades
notre, nos our
nous we
nouveau (nouvel, nouvelle, nouveaux) new
novembre November; **en novembre** in November
la **nuit** night

obéir to obey; **obéir à quelqu'un** to obey someone
octobre October; **en octobre** in October
l' **œuf** *(masc.)* egg
offrir *(irreg.)* to offer, give something as a gift
on people, one; *(colloq.)* we
l' **oncle** *(masc.)* uncle
onze eleven
optimiste optimistic
l' **orange** *(fem.)* orange; **l'orange pressée** orange drink, orangeade
orange *(invariable)* orange; orange-colored
l' **ordinateur** *(masc.)* computer
où where
oublier to forget
ouvert open
ouvrir *(irreg.)* to open

le **pain** bread
le **palais** palace
le **pantalon** pants
le **papier** paper, piece of paper
le **parapluie** umbrella
le **parc** park
les **parents** *(masc. pl.)* parents; relatives
paresseux(-se) lazy
le **parking** parking lot
parler to speak
le **parquet** floor, wood flooring
partager (g ➤ ge/a,o) to share
partir *(irreg., passé composé with être)* to leave, set out
partout everywhere
le **passager** passenger
passer to spend time
passer un examen to take, have a test

les **passe-temps** free time
passionnant exciting
le **pâté** pâté, goose liver pâté
les **pâtes** *(fem. pl.)* pasta
patient patient
payer (y ➤ i/mute e) to pay
les **Pays-Bas** *(masc. pl.)* The Netherlands
la **pêche** peach
pendant during
la **penderie** (walk-in) closet
pénible annoying
penser to think
perdre to lose; **perdre son temps** to waste one's time
le **père** father
la **permanence** study hall
personne nobody
péruvien(ne) Peruvian
pessimiste pessimistic
petit small, little, short
le **petit déjeuner** breakfast
les **petits pois** *(masc. pl.)* peas
peu de little, few, not much, not many
la **philosophie** philosophy
la **photo** photograph, picture
la **physique** physics
la **pièce** room
pile sharp *(said of time)*
la **piscine** swimming pool
la **pizza** pizza
le **placard** closet, cupboard
pleuvoir to rain; **il pleut** it's raining
la **pluie** rain
plus no more, no longer
la **poire** pear
le **poisson** fish; **Poisson d'avril!** April fool!
poli polite
poliment politely
la **pomme** apple
la **pomme de terre** potato
la **porte** door; gate
porter to carry; to wear
portugais Portuguese; **le portugais** Portuguese *(language)*
le **Portugal** Portugal
poser une question to ask a question
le **poste de télé** TV set
le **poulet** chicken
pour for, in order to
pourquoi? why?; **pourquoi pas?** why not?
pousser to grow *(said of plants)*
pouvoir *(irreg.)* to be able
préférer (je préfère) to prefer
prendre *(irreg.)* to take; to have *(something to eat or drink)*
prendre dans ses bras to pick up
prendre des billets to buy tickets
prendre rendez-vous to make an appointment
préparer to prepare
près de near
présenter to present, to introduce
presque almost
pressé in a hurry
prêt *(fem. prête)* ready

prêter to loan
le printemps spring; au printemps in the spring
la prise taking, capture
prochain next
le produit product
le prof teacher (familiar)
le professeur teacher (male or female)
le programmeur (la programmeuse) programmer
les projets (masc. pl.) plans
prononcer (c ≻ ç/a,o) to pronounce
la prononciation pronunciation
proposer to suggest
la prune plum
le pull sweater
le pupitre student's desk
la psychologie psychology

quand? when?
quarante forty
le quart quarter
le quartier neighborhood
quatorze fourteen
quatre four
quatre-vingt-dix ninety
quatre-vingts eighty
quel(le)(s) which
quelque chose something
quelquefois sometimes
quelqu'un somebody, someone
qu'est-ce que? what?
la question question
qui? who? (subject of the verb)
qui est-ce que? whom? (object of the verb)
quinze fifteen
quitter to leave

raccompagner to walk (someone) home
raccrocher to hang up
raconter to tell, narrate
le raisin grapes
raisonnable sensible
ranger (g ≻ ge/a,o) to put away (one's belongings)
rapporter to bring back
rarement seldom
le rasoir électrique electric shaver
récemment recently
la recette recipe
recopier to copy, write out
rédiger (g ≻ ge/a,o) to draft, write
réfléchir to think over, reflect
regarder to look at
le régime diet
remarquer to notice
remplacer (c ≻ ç/a,o) to replace
rencontrer to meet (by chance)
le rendez-vous appointment, date, meeting
rendre to give back; rendre visite à to visit (someone)
rentrer to go back, go home
le repas meal
répéter (je répète) to repeat
le répondeur answering machine
répondre to answer

la réponse answer
la république republic
rester (passé composé with être) to stay, remain;
    rester ouvert to remain open
retrouver to meet (customarily or by appointment)
réussir to succeed, pass a test; ne pas réussir to fail
    a test
rêver to dream, to daydream
réviser to review
la revue magazine
le rez-de-chaussée ground floor
rien nothing
le riz rice
la robe dress
le roi king
le roman novel; le roman d'aventures adventure novel
rose pink
rouge red
la ruine ruin
russe Russian; le russe Russian (language)

le sac à dos backpack
le sac de couchage sleeping bag
sage: être sage to be good (said of children)
la saison season
la salade lettuce, salad
la salle à manger dining room
la salle de bains bathroom
la salle de classe classroom
la salle de réunion auditorium, meeting room
la salle de séjour living room
le salon living room
saluer to greet, say hello to
samedi Saturday; le samedi on Saturdays
les sandales (fem. pl.) sandals
le saucisson sausage, salami
savoir (irreg.) to know (information)
le saxophone saxophone
les sciences (fem. pl.) science
le sèche-cheveux hair dryer
le secrétaire; la secrétaire secretary
seize sixteen
la semaine prochaine next week
le sénat senate
le Sénégal Senegal
sept seven
septembre September; en septembre in September
sérieux(-se) serious
le serveur waiter; (la serveuse) waitress
la serviette briefcase; bath towel
servir (irreg.) to serve
le short shorts
six six
la sociologie sociology
la sœur sister
soigneusement carefully
le soir evening; ce soir this evening
la soirée evening, evening hours
soixante sixty
soixante-dix seventy
son, sa, ses his, her, its
sonner to ring

la   **sortie** evening out; exit; leaving; **à la sortie de l'école** when school lets out
     sortir (*irreg.,* **passé composé** *with* **être**) to go out
     sous under
le   **sous-sol** basement
     souvent often
le   **sport** sport
     sportif (*fem.* **sportive**) athletic
le   **stade** stadium
le   **stylo** pen; **stylo à bille** ballpoint pen
le   **sucre** sugar
le   **sud** south; **au sud de** to the south of
     suédois Swedish
     suisse Swiss
     sur on
la   **surboum** party
le   **surligneur** highlighter
     sympathique nice, pleasant

la   **table** table
le   **tableau** chalkboard; picture
     tant de so much, so many
la   **tante** aunt
     tard late
la   **tarte** type of pastry resembling a pie; **tarte aux poires** pear tart; **tarte aux pommes** apple tart
la   **tasse** cup
le   **taxi** taxi
le   **tee-shirt** tee shirt
     téléphoner to call, phone
     tellement so
le   **terrain de sport** athletic field
le   **TGV** high speed train
le   **thé** tea; **le thé glacé** iced tea
le   **théâtre** theater
le   **thème** subject
     timide shy
le   **tiroir** drawer
     toi (*stressed pronoun*) you
les   **toilettes** (*fem. pl.*) toilet, restroom
la   **tomate** tomato
     ton, ta, tes your
     tôt early
la   **touche** key (*computer*)
     toujours always
le   **touriste, la touriste** tourist
     tous les jours every day
     tout de suite right away
     tout d'un coup all of a sudden
     tout le monde everyone
     toute la journée all day long
     toutes les semaines every week
le   **train** train
     tranquille calm
le   **travail** work
     travailler to work, study; **travailler dur** to work, study hard
     travailleur (*fem.* **travailleuse**) hard-working
     treize thirteen
     trente thirty
     trois three
le   **trombone** paper clip; trombone

     trop de too much, too many
le   **trottoir** sidewalk
     trouver to find
     tu (*informal singular*) you
la   **Tunisie** Tunisia
     tunisien(ne) Tunisian
     tutoyer (**y ➤ i/mute e**) to use the **tu** form to address someone

     un, une one, a, an
     un peu de a little
l'   **université** (*fem.*) university
     utiliser to use

la   **vache** cow
la   **valise** suitcase
le   **veau** veal
la   **veille** the evening before, the day before
le   **vélo** bike
le   **vendeur (la vendeuse)** salesclerk
     vendre to sell
     vendredi Friday; **le vendredi** on Fridays
     vénézuélien(ne) Venezuelan
     venir (*irreg.*) to come
le   **verbe** verb
le   **verger** orchard
la   **vérité** truth
le   **verre** glass
     vers toward
     vert green
la   **veste** jacket
les   **vêtements** (*masc. pl.*) clothing
la   **viande** meat
la   **vie** life
     vieux (vieil, vieille, vieux) old
la   **vigne** grapevine
le   **vignoble** vineyard
la   **ville** city, town; **en ville** downtown, in town
le   **vin** wine
     vingt twenty
     violet (*fem.* **violette**) violet, purple
le   **violon** violin
la   **vitrine** shop window
     voici here is, here are
     voilà there is, there are
     voir (*irreg.*) to see; **C'est un film à voir.** It's a film worth seeing; **voir la vie en rose** to take a rosy view of things; **voir la vie en noir** to take a negative view of things
la   **voiture** car
     votre, vos your
     vouloir (*irreg.*) to want
     vous you (*formal singular and plural*)
     vouvoyer (**y ➤ i/mute e**) to use the **vous** form to address someone
le   **voyage** trip; **le voyage scolaire** school trip
     voyager to travel
le   **voyageur; la voyageuse** traveler
     vraiment really, truly

     zéro zero
le   **zoo** zoo

INDEX